DENMARK

Robert Pateman

MARSHALL CAVENDISH
New York • London • Sydney

Reference edition published 1995 by
Marshall Cavendish Corporation
2415 Jerusalem Avenue
P.O. Box 587
North Bellmore
New York 11710

© Times Editions Pte Ltd 1995

Originated and designed by
Times Books International, an imprint of
Times Editions Pte Ltd

Printed in Singapore

Library of Congress Cataloging-in-Publication Data:
Pateman, Robert.
    Denmark / Robert Pateman.
        p. cm.—(Cultures Of The World)
    Includes bibliographical references and index.
    Summary: Introduces the geography, history,
economics, culture, and people of the country of Denmark.
    ISBN 0-7614-0168-7 (Denmark)
    ISBN 0-7614-0167-9 (Set)
    1. Denmark—Juvenile literature. [1. Denmark] I. Title.
II. Series.
DL109.P37 1995
948.9—dc20   94–43340
                    CIP
                    AC

Cultures of the World

Editorial Director	Shirley Hew
Managing Editor	Shova Loh
Editors	Elizabeth Berg
	Dinah Lee
	Azra Moiz
	Sue Sismondo
Picture Editor	Susan Jane Manuel
Production	Anthoney Chua
Design	Tuck Loong
	Felicia Wong
	Loo Chuan Ming
	Wendy Koh
Illustrators	Chow Kok Keong
	Anuar bin Abdul Rahim
MCC Editorial Director	Evelyn M. Fazio

INTRODUCTION

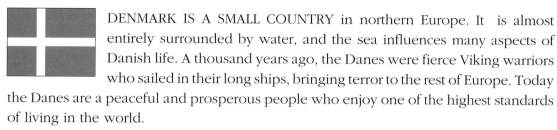 DENMARK IS A SMALL COUNTRY in northern Europe. It is almost entirely surrounded by water, and the sea influences many aspects of Danish life. A thousand years ago, the Danes were fierce Viking warriors who sailed in their long ships, bringing terror to the rest of Europe. Today the Danes are a peaceful and prosperous people who enjoy one of the highest standards of living in the world.

Denmark conjures up many different images: the Little Mermaid Statue in Copenhagen, rolling farmland, the royal guards in their immaculate red uniforms. Behind these visual symbols of the nation lies a more private side of Denmark that is more difficult to explore. A sense of humor, close family ties, national pride, and happy evenings spent enjoying good food with friends are equally important elements of the Danish culture.

CONTENTS

A Danish symbol of manual labor includes a windmill and Danish flag.

CONTENTS

A street painting in Copenhagen.

GEOGRAPHY

DENMARK IS A SMALL COUNTRY in northern Europe. It covers 16,639 square miles (43,094 sq km), which is about twice the size of Massachusetts. It is made up of the narrow Jutland Peninsula and over 400 islands. Nowhere in Denmark is farther than 32 miles (52 km) from the sea.

Jutland is joined to mainland Europe by a 42-mile (67 km) land border with Germany. It makes up about two-thirds of the total land area of Denmark. The soil here is generally of poor quality and long ago was covered with moor, heath, and sand dunes. Today the use of modern fertilizers allows extensive farming to take place.

The islands are generally far more fertile, with the most typical features being low rolling hills, lakes, and beaches. The Danish capital, Copenhagen, is situated on the island of Zealand.

Denmark's history has been strongly influenced by its geography. An agriculturally poor land surrounded by the sea, its people have always been drawn to sailing. Situated between Europe and the Baltic countries, it has served as a link between these two regions.

Opposite: **One of the many rivers in the beautiful Faeroe Islands.**

Left: **Denmark was once covered with deciduous forest, such as Rold Forest.**

Rolling hills line a beach in northern Zealand.

The longest river in Denmark is the Gudenå, which starts in central Jutland and enters the sea on the east coast. However, even the Gudenå is less than 100 miles long.

PHYSICAL FEATURES

Denmark is a flat country. This is the result of the glaciers that pushed across the land during the ice ages. Undulating plains alternate with gently rolling hills. A line of low hills running north to south through the Jutland Peninsula clearly marks the farthest point of the most recent glacier advance. The highest point, Yding Skovhøj in East Jutland, is 568 feet (173 m) above sea level. Another legacy of the ice ages is the countless small lakes and streams. Arresø in North Zealand is the biggest of the lakes, covering 15.7 square miles (40.8 sq km).

Dune landscapes form an almost unbroken belt along the west coast of Jutland. The western dune coast has many sandy beaches and *fjords* ("fee-YORDS"). The calm waters of the fjords make them favorite places for Denmark's yachts. There are two major fjords, Lim Fjord in Jutland and Ise Fjord in Zealand. The long Danish coastline has a great number of gulfs, inlets, and lagoons that contain brackish (somewhat salty) water.

NORWAY

SKAGERRAK

KATTEGAT STRAIT

FAEROE ISLANDS

Nissum Bredning

Løgstør Bredning

Lim Fjord

Randers Fjord

Gudenå R.

JUTLAND PENINSULA

Ringkøbing Fjord

Yding Skovhøj

Lake Arresø

SWEDEN

ØRESUND

FANO I.

Odense Fjord

GREAT BELT

ZEALAND I.

AMAGER I.

NORTH SEA

FYN I.

LITTLE BELT

BORNHOLM I.

GERMANY

AERO I.

LANGELAND I.

LOLLAND I.

Møns Klint

MØN I.

FALSTER I.

The northern flat plains are a fertile area that was once under the sea. The east central hills are also fertile, with low hills and many inlets.

THE CLIMATE

Denmark's climate is strongly influenced by the sea. Thanks to the warm North Atlantic Drift, which is part of the Gulf Stream, the weather is often mild for a country at such a high latitude. Being surrounded by water means Denmark receives a heavy rainfall, averaging about 25 inches a year. Jutland is generally the wettest part of the country; the area can receive over 30 inches of annual precipitation.

The lack of mountains is another strong influence on the weather. It means that winds blowing in from the sea can quickly sweep across the whole country. As a result, it is unusual to find the weather differing very much from one part of Denmark to another.

FLORA AND FAUNA

Most of Denmark was originally covered by deciduous forest, the most common trees being beech, oak, elm, and lime. Virtually all the original forest was chopped down several centuries ago. Today approximately 12 percent of Denmark is covered with trees, but these are mostly replanted forests. In Jutland many of the new plantations are of coniferous trees such as spruce and fir, which grow in areas that were once open heath.

Such drastic human interference has had a major effect on the wildlife, and over the centuries many mammal species have disappeared from Denmark. These include bear, boar, wolves, and elk, some of which have found a shelter in the more northerly regions of Scandinavia. Today the largest mammal in Denmark is the red deer. Smaller mammals are still common and include several species of bats, red squirrels, hares, and hedgehogs.

Denmark is home to around 300 species of birds. The long coastline with its many inlets and gulfs provides a particularly rich home for water birds, including herons, swans, and storks. Storks play an important role in Danish folklore and are believed to bring good luck. Although they are strictly protected, their numbers continue to decline.

Denmark is home in the summer months to a surprising number of butterflies, many of which migrate from the Mediterranean.

The seas around Denmark are an important breeding ground for fish, with abundant cod, herring, and plaice. The waters are also rich in sea mammals, including dolphins, porpoises, and seals.

Today most Danes have a good understanding of environmental problems, and Denmark has made excellent progress in reducing pollution and recycling resources.

This red squirrel must hibernate to avoid the harsh Danish winter.

FOUR SEASONS

Denmark has four distinct seasons, which many Danes feel contributes to the beauty of their country. Spring starts in March and lasts to May. In early May, the beech tree, the national tree of Denmark, comes into leaf.

Summer has temperatures of 67–70°F (19–21°C) on the hottest days. Summer also brings 17.5 hours of daylight, so that it does not get dark until after 9 p.m. in the evening. Indeed, at the height of summer the night sky never seems to get completely dark. The summer months are also the wettest, and several days in a row might bring gray skies and rain.

The first signs of autumn appear around September; by October the forests are brown, as trees shed their leaves in preparation for the coming winter.

In a typical year, Denmark might receive 120 days of freezing weather. On the average there are between 20 and 30 days of snow, although snowfall is not guaranteed and will certainly not be as heavy as in Norway or Sweden to the north. Indeed, the last few years have brought a spell of exceptionally mild winters.

Springtime is a beautiful time to be in the country-side, when the fields are alive with flowers.

Denmark gets around seven hours of sunlight in winter, and it is dark when people leave for work and dark when they start their journey home. This, perhaps even more than the cold, has a tremendous influence on the Danish lifestyle.

11

A house with a turf roof in the Faeroe Islands.

Greenland and the Faeroe Islands are self-governing regions that are still possessions of Denmark.

FAEROE ISLANDS

The Faeroes are a group of islands in the North Atlantic, almost halfway between northern Europe and Iceland. They are made of volcanic rock, with peaks rising to nearly 3,000 feet (900 m).

The North Atlantic Drift keeps the temperature remarkably mild for such a northerly position, but the Faeroes receive heavy rainfall and fierce storms and are often covered by a thick blanket of fog and mist. The summer months produce at least a few hot and clear days.

Their northerly position means that during winter the Faeroes only receive a few hours of sunlight each day. In contrast, summer days are long and the nights very short.

Seventeen of the approximately 22 islands are inhabited, and the total population is nearly 50,000. Fishing occupies over a quarter of the work force, so declining fish stocks have created a serious threat to the economy. The Faeroes are now deeply in debt and require a heavy annual grant from the Danish government.

KALAALLIT NUNAAT
(Greenland)

White indicates areas covered by ice cap.

GREENLAND

Greenland is the world's largest island. It lies 2,000 miles (600 m) north of Denmark and is surrounded by the cold North Atlantic and Arctic Oceans, giving it an arctic climate. It is so cold in the interior that the snow never melts. Instead one layer of snow is compressed into ice by the weight of subsequent snowfalls. Eighty-five percent of the island lies beneath this permanent ice cap, which is up to 5,000 feet (1,500 m) deep. Glaciers are pushed down from the ice cap into the fjords below. The Jacobshaven Glacier can move as much as 30 feet (9 m) a day.

Despite these inhospitable conditions, rich stocks of fish, birds, and sea mammals encouraged early human hunters to brave the icy environment. Today Greenland's population is concentrated along the ice-free coastal areas of the southwest. Fishing is the main industry, with a small number of people in the far south making a living as shepherds or cattle farmers. There is some exploration work going on, and the Danish government is searching for offshore oil.

Greenland is considered part of the North American continent but is politically part of Denmark.

Nyhavn Harbor cuts through the center of Copenhagen.

COPENHAGEN

Copenhagen, or København in Danish, is Denmark's capital city. It has a population of approximately half a million people, but including the heavily built up surrounding areas raises this figure to around 1.3 million, or nearly a quarter of the total Danish population. Despite its size, Copenhagen remains a pleasant, safe, and clean city.

Copenhagen was founded around 800 years ago by Bishop Absalon. It did not become the capital until 1443, but after that, it quickly grew into the cultural and political center of the country. The next 200 years saw the construction of many of the grand buildings that give the city center its special character today.

Over the centuries, Copenhagen has survived wars, plagues, and fires. The destructive fires of 1728 and 1795 allowed the planners to redesign the city and create many of today's boulevards, parks, and gardens.

By the start of this century, Copenhagen had become the center of Denmark's industrial growth, bringing new prosperity. The city is famous for its breweries and porcelain factories, but these are actually less important to the economy than the engineering, clothing, and food processing industries.

Recent changes include removing the old tramway and turning the center of the city into a pedestrian area. Kastrup Airport, just a few miles from the city center, has grown into one of the busiest airports in Europe.

OTHER CITIES

Apart from Copenhagen, the rest of Denmark's cities have more the atmosphere of small towns.

Århus is the second largest city. It is located in east Jutland and traces its history back to a Viking settlement. Today it is an important industrial center and has a major commercial college in addition to a school of journalism. Many people find the pace of life here more relaxing than in Copenhagen.

Odense lies on the island of Fyn at the center of some of Denmark's richest farmland. Although it is a major industrial city and shipbuilding center, the city center still has many beautiful old buildings. These include the childhood home of Hans Christian Andersen, now one of Denmark's finest museums.

Ålborg, in North Jutland, is the fourth largest Danish city. A bridge across the River Limford joins it with the residential areas on the northern bank, which are now considered part of greater Ålborg. There are important brick and cement industries that use local clay and chalk, and the modern port is the main link with Greenland. The city has its own zoo and Tivoli Park.

Copenhagen is Denmark's leading port, as well as being its industrial, educational, and cultural center.

15

HISTORY

THERE IS EVIDENCE THAT people were living in Denmark as long ago as 50,000 B.C., but these primitive hunters were driven out by the last ice age. Nomadic tribes returned with the warmer weather and resettled the area around 14,000 years ago. This was the Stone Age, when people used flint to produce high-quality tools and weapons.

The period around 1500 B.C. brought two major technological advances: farming was transformed by the invention of the wooden plow, and people learned to make metal tools from cooper and bronze. As the Danish tribes became richer, important trading links were established with the more advanced nations to the south.

We know very little about the politics of the time, but the land was probably divided into small tribal areas, each ruled by a local chieftain. It was not until around A.D. 400 that larger villages appeared. These are the first signs that political power was starting to concentrate in the hands of a few individuals.

The artwork that found its way to Denmark along the Mediterranean trade routes inspired local artists to produce some excellent work of their own. One of the most wonderful pieces produced in this early period is the bronze age model of a sun chariot from Trundholm, which can now be seen in the National Museum.

Opposite: **Frederiksborg Castle was originally a small country home. Christian IV rebuilt it into a palace in the 1600s.**

Left: **An important change occurred about 4000 B.C., when people learned to clear the forests and settle in one area as farmers. These first farming communities built the large stone tombs that can still be seen in the Danish countryside.**

The European imagination is still inspired by the exploits of the Viking warriors. The well-known double-horned helmet is probably not accurate.

THE VIKING PERIOD

From the ninth to the 11th centuries, Viking warriors from Denmark and the other Scandinavian countries raided much of Europe, bringing terror wherever they sailed. The first record of a Viking raid dates to 793, when warriors attacked the English monastery of Lindisfarne. They took the little community by surprise, plundering the church and killing the monks or carrying them off.

We cannot be certain what social or political changes provoked these raids, but one major factor might well have been a growth in population that left many people without sufficient farmland.

At first the Vikings made only brief raids, burning small villages and then fleeing back to the sea. However, the death of King Charlemagne of France in 814 weakened mainland Europe and allowed the Vikings to become bolder. Danish Vikings were soon sailing up the major rivers of Europe to plunder cities in England, France, and Germany. Raiding eventually gave way to conquest and by 878 a Danish Grand Army had seized a large part of eastern England. In 911 the King of France gave the province of Normandy to the Viking chieftain Rollo in return for Rollo's protection.

In 1013 King Canute of Denmark subjugated all of England. Danish kings occupied the throne of England until the death of King Harthacnut in 1042. That year is considered to end the Viking period, although Duke William the Conqueror of Normandy, who in 1066 conquered England, was a direct descendent of the Viking chieftain Rollo.

LIFE IN A VIKING SOCIETY

A typical Viking home had one large building with a single room where both people and animals slept. This was made from timber and stone and had wattle and daub walls. There was very little furniture inside the house. The head of the house might have a bed and a chair, but the rest of the family slept on mats that were laid out on the floor each night. Valuables were stored in wooden chests, but most objects were hung on the walls. A fire pit in the middle of the room was used for cooking and heating. Despite an opening in the roof, this must have made the houses smoky.

Most Danes at this time lived either on isolated farms or in small villages, but there were also a few larger settlements. Hedeby was a particularly wealthy trading town at the foot of the Jutland Peninsula. The sites of several large fortified camps have also been discovered.

During the Viking period, Denmark was primarily an agricultural country. Vikings cultivated barley, rye, oats, and wheat. Farmers kept cattle, pigs, horses, sheep, and goats. Warriors were recruited from the farmers.

The first mention of Ribe dates from 862, when the town was a well-organized trade center where markets were held regularly.

Wattle and daub was used for making the walls of most Viking buildings. Wattle was a frame made from weaving thin tree branches together. These were then covered with daub—a paste made from straw, mud, and cow dung.

19

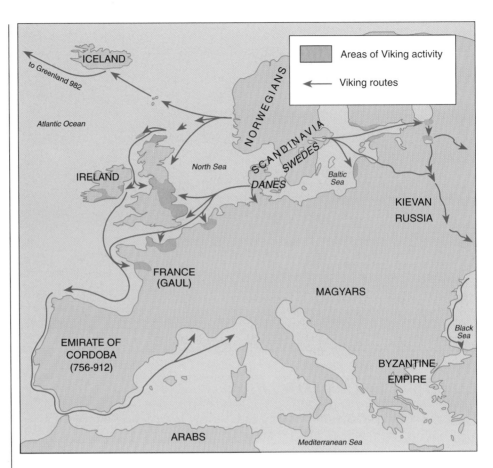

Viking ships often sailed with mixed crews, the warriors coming from all parts of the Scandinavian region. However, evidence suggests that most of the raids on southern England were the work of Vikings from Denmark, while Norwegian Vikings played the major role in attacks on Scotland and Ireland.

EXPLORERS OF THE SEA

Sailing in their open wooden boats, the Vikings explored the coastline of Europe and navigated down the great Russian rivers. Other ships ventured west into the dangerous North Atlantic, where they colonized Iceland and Greenland. Leif Erikson and his crew sailed even farther, exploring the shores of North America in A.D. 1000.

The Nordic shipbuilders designed craft that were both light and strong. Their ships tapered at both ends and were steered by a single rudder placed at the stern. The ships were driven by a large, square sail, but could also be rowed. The long ship was a battle craft carrying up to 40 warriors. It could be over 90 feet in length and was low and narrow. Merchant ships, in contrast, were tall and wide and had a covered deck.

A WONDERFUL FIND

An old tradition claimed that a galleon had been sunk in the Roskilde Fjord to block one channel and protect the town of Roskilde from raids. When divers explored the sea bed, they found the remains of five ships. More importantly, the find was much older than people had expected and dated to the Viking period.

An iron enclosure was placed around the wrecks, and the water was pumped out. Hundreds of years on the sea bottom had flattened the craft and their timber was rotten and crumbling. Over 50,000 separate pieces of wood were discovered, each of which had to be carefully dried out and preserved. The remains of the ships were reassembled piece by piece.

Two of the craft were warships, including a 40-warrior long ship, but there were also two merchant ships and a small fishing or ferry boat. Today the Roskilde ships are housed in a modern museum built on the edge of the fjord.

The name Viking appears on early runic stones, and was always used in connection with sea battles. The fierce sailors in their long ships were also known as Norsemen, Northmen, *or* Danes. *The Franks called them* Ascomans *or* Normanni; *and the Arabs,* Rus *or* al-Magus.

This nice bedroom in Frederiksborg Castle is decorated in the style of the 17th century.

A BALTIC POWER

Denmark had entered the Viking period as a little-known collection of tribes on the edge of Europe. It emerged three centuries later as a powerful nation, united under one king, that had extended its influence over much of the Baltic Sea region.

Valdemar I, who came to the throne in 1157, was the greatest king of the new age. With the assistance of Bishop Absalon he restored Denmark's declining military power and established schools, fortresses, churches, and monasteries throughout the country. About half the modern cities in Denmark, including Copenhagen, were founded during Valdemar's reign.

Around 1240 a series of weak kings conceded power to the nobles and clergy, and Denmark suffered a long period of civil war. It was over a century before Valdemar IV reunited the country. His daughter, Queen Margrethe, united Denmark, Sweden, and Norway in the Union of Kalmar in 1397. Copenhagen became the political and cultural center of the region. Sweden broke away from the union in 1523, but Norway was ruled by Denmark for the next three hundred years.

The breakup of the union left Denmark and Sweden as regional rivals and led to a series of wars. The Danes lost most of their territory to the Swedish during the war of 1657-1660. In 1700 they attempted to regain this lost territory, but although the Great Northern War dragged on for over 20 years it achieved little.

In 1536 King Christian III converted Denmark from a Catholic to a Protestant nation.

THE LOSS OF AN EMPIRE

The 18th and 19th centuries saw a new balance of power in Europe force Denmark into further conflicts. Denmark tried to stay neutral in the Napoleonic Wars, but in 1807 the British bombarded Copenhagen and captured most of the Danish navy. Denmark then formed an alliance with France and as a result lost possession of Norway after the French defeat.

In 1848 a revolution broke out in the provinces of Schleswig and Holstein. These were ruled by the Danish king, but were not part of Denmark. The rebels wanted to end Danish rule and join the German Confederation. Danish troops put down the revolution, but when they tried to make Schleswig part of Denmark, Prussia intervened. In 1864 Prussian and Austrian troops invaded Denmark and after a quick victory took over both Schleswig and Holstein.

In 1866 Enrico Dalgas, a young road engineer, found a way to reclaim land from the sea by draining marshes and planting evergreen trees to hold the soil. This land reclamation was so extensive that it made up for the loss of Schleswig and Holstein.

Eighteenth-century houses in the center of Copenhagen.

Today Denmark has many dairy farms, because many farmers switched from growing grain to raising livestock in the late 19th century.

The 1930s saw the birth of the Danish welfare state, with the introduction of benefits such as retirement pensions and health coverage. This was an important step toward creating the modern Danish society.

SOCIAL CHANGES

While Denmark's military power was declining, important social and economic reforms were taking place at home. The latter part of the 18th century brought the abolition of serfdom. Important land reforms followed that enabled farmers to buy the land they worked. This gave people the taste for freedom, and in 1849 King Frederick VII was forced to accept a democratic constitution that established a new parliament.

The 19th century saw considerable growth in trade and industry. At the same time, farmers improved their efficiency by organizing themselves into cooperatives. Despite such progress, there was a major economic depression at the end of the century. In particular, farmers were badly hit, and many left to seek a better life in the United States. Those who stayed responded to the crisis by switching from growing grain to keeping livestock. This move laid the foundation of the modern farming industry.

In 1915 a new constitution ended the special rights of the upper class, laying the basis for modern Denmark's democratic society.

WORLD WAR II AND AFTER

The decade of the 1930s was a difficult period for the country, particularly the farmers, who were badly hit by the world depression. At the same time, Hitler's rise to power in Germany cast a threatening cloud over Europe. In 1939 Denmark signed a pact with Germany, promising neither country would attack the other. When war broke out in Europe a few months later, Danes did not expect their country to be directly involved. However, on April 9, 1940, German troops made a surprise attack on Denmark, overcoming Danish resistance in a few hours.

At first the Danes were allowed to retain their own government, but as the war dragged on, German rule became harsher and Danish resistance stronger. Trains and factories were sabotaged and in August 1943 the German army took over the running of the country. When the Germans attempted to deport Denmark's Jewish population, the Danes responded by hiding most of the country's Jewish families until they could be smuggled to safety in Sweden.

Denmark came out of the war with relatively little damage to its cities or industry, and the 1950s brought dramatic growth in the nation's wealth. In the postwar period Denmark has tightened ties with the rest of Europe. Denmark became a member of the North Atlantic Treaty Organization (NATO) in 1949 and in 1973 joined the European Common Market.

Another postwar challenge has been to redefine the role of former colonies. Iceland was granted independence in 1945, while the Faeroe Islands and Greenland were granted home rule in 1948 and 1979 respectively. Under the Home Rule Act, the areas of justice, finance, defense, and foreign relations are the responsibility of the Danish government, while education, health, and social services are jointly administered.

Environmental concerns were a major issue during the mid-1980s. In 1987 Denmark's parliament passed very strong evironmental protection laws.

GOVERNMENT

DENMARK IS A CONSTITUTIONAL MONARCHY, with the queen as chief of state. The present ruler is Queen Margrethe II. Denmark has the oldest unbroken royal line in Europe; its royal family dates to King Gorm in 930. Today, however, the prime minister is the actual head of government.

The prime minister is the leader of the majority party or, as is usually the case in Denmark, a coalition of parties. One of the prime minister's most important jobs is to form the cabinet. Most members of the cabinet oversee one area of government. They also advise the prime minister during cabinet meetings.

Parliament has a single chamber called the *Folketing* ("folk-keh-TING"). It has 179 elected members, including two from Greenland and two from the Faeroe Islands.

Every Dane over 18 is entitled to vote, and Danish people take politics seriously. The normal turnout is over 90 percent of the eligible population.

There is proportional representation with a two percent limit. This means that any party gaining more than two percent of the total vote is guaranteed seats in parliament. The usual outcome of this system is that many different parties are represented in the Folketing, so that a majority can only be achieved if several parties join together in a coalition.

The parliament frequently uses referendums. If one-third of the members of parliament call for a referendum, that issue must be put to the population. This allows the public to vote on important or controversial decisions. In recent years, issues such as joining the European Community and lowering the voting age have been decided by referendum.

The current prime minister is Poul Rasmussen of the Social Democratic Party. He leads a coalition with the Radical Liberals, the Center Democrats, and the Christian People's Party. Formed in February 1994, this is the first majority government in Denmark in 11 years, controlling 90 of the 179 seats in the legislature.

The Danish flag of a white cross on a red background is the oldest national flag in the world. We know for certain that it was used by King Valdemar IV, who ruled in the middle of the 14th century. However, according to legend it is over a hundred years older than this, having fallen from the sky at the Battle of Lyndanisse as a sign for the Danish army.

Opposite: **Guards at Amalienborg Palace wear uniforms from the 19th century.**

Copenhagen Town Hall. Each county or municipality has an elected council headed by a mayor.

If anybody feels they have been unfairly treated by local government officials, they can appeal to the ombudsman, who reports directly to the Folketing.

THE STRUCTURE OF GOVERNMENT

At present there are 21 ministries, each in charge of a different area of government. These include Foreign Affairs, Justice, Social and Cultural Affairs, and State Finances. In recent years, a Ministry of the Environment has been formed to deal with areas such as pollution. The Ministry of Energy oversees the important North Sea gas and oil resources.

Each ministry is headed by a member of the cabinet. However, civil servants within the ministry do not change when there is a new government. Instead they are expected to be loyal to the government in power.

For local government and administration, Denmark is divided into 14 counties and two municipalities (Copenhagen and Frederiksberg). The counties are further divided into municipalities, each with an elected municipal board. A municipality usually consists of an urban center and the surrounding rural area.

The county authorities are responsible for major roads, hospitals, and secondary schools within their area. The municipal boards are in charge of water, gas, electric supplies, social welfare, primary schools, libraries, and minor roads.

THE PARLIAMENT BUILDING

Denmark is governed from Slotsholmen Island in the very center of Copenhagen. The Folketing is housed there in Christiansborg Palace, one of the most beautiful parliament buildings in the world. This grand U-shaped building with its distinctive tower was built at the turn of the century. A statue of King Frederick VII, who established the modern parliament, stands in front of the building.

Most ministries are located on the island. Several, including the important Finance Ministry, are housed in the Red Building, which is nearly 300 years old. Recently the Foreign Ministry decided there was no longer adequate room on Slotsholmen, and they opened additional offices in another part of the city. This is a trend that other ministries will no doubt be forced to follow in the future.

THE EUROPEAN UNION

In 1973 Denmark entered the European Community. In February, 1992, the Maastricht Treaty was formulated, changing the European Community to the European Union. The European Union envisages broad changes in the relations of its members, including the evolution of a supranational federal Europe with a full monetary union, a common currency, and the removal of all trade barriers.

In May 1992, the Folketing voted to approve the Maastricht Treaty. In a referendum held in June, however, 50.7 percent of the Danish voters were against ratification. In subsequent negotiations Denmark was given an exemption from certain provisions of the treaty, including the adoption of a single currency, participation in a common defense policy, common European citizenship, and cooperation in legal and home affairs. In a second referendum in May 1993, 56.7 percent of the voters were in favor of ratification.

Seats in parliament:
- *135 seats for winners of electoral districts.*
- *40 seats reserved for parties who win over two percent of votes nationwide but do not gain a fair proportion of seats in the Folketing.*
- *Two seats for Greenland.*
- *Two seats for Faeroes.*

Ålborg town hall.

The current administration has adopted measures aimed at reducing the rate of unemployment, which currently affects 12 percent of the workforce.

THE PARTIES

Before 1960 Danish politics were dominated by "the four old parties." These still exist, although they have had to change and adapt to new trends.

The four old parties are:

The Social Democratic Party (*Social-demokratiet*) is historically the most successful party in Danish politics. It traditionally enjoys the support of the trade unions.

The Conservative People's Party (*Det Konservative Folkeparti*) is usually considered the party of businesspeople or higher-ranking government employees.

The Liberal Party (*Venstre Danmarks Liberale Parti*) counts on the vote of the farming community but has also gained considerable support in urban areas.

The Radical Liberal Party (*Det Radikale Venstre*) is the smallest of the four old parties, supported by a section of the farming community and university people.

The Socialist People's Party was the first to break this pattern when it won several seats in the 1960 election. The 1973 elections radically altered the shape of the Danish political scene. Eleven parties won a place in parliament, and five parties who had never been represented in parliament suddenly found themselves sharing a third of the seats.

The new forces in Danish politics include the Socialist People's Party, the Progress Party, the Center Democrats, and the Christian People's Party.

Poul Schlüter's Conservative People's Party held power from 1982 until 1994, when the conservatives were replaced by the Social Democrats.

MARGRETHE II, DENMARK'S QUEEN

When Germany invaded Denmark in April 1940, King Christian X, the present queen's grandfather, decided that the royal family would remain in Copenhagen to share the hardships and dangers with their people. Queen Margrethe was born in Amalienborg Castle just a few days after the invasion. Her birth gave the Danes something to celebrate at this terrible moment in their history.

In 1953, when it was clear there would not be a male heir, new laws were passed to allow female succession to the throne. Margrethe was carefully educated in politics, economics, and history at the university. In June 1967 Margrethe married Count Henri de Laborde, a French diplomat. The couple now have two sons, Prince Frederik (born in 1968), and Prince Joachim, who is a year younger.

Queen Margrethe came to the throne in January 1972 at the age of 31. She has used her influence as queen to encourage her people to improve themselves, particularly in her New Year's Eve address. In 1987 she criticized her listeners for their lack of initiative: "This attitude is very familiar: it's a don't-get-too-uppity attitude, don't get too big for your boots—keep your head down, nobody will notice you. It's perhaps not untypical of village life anywhere, but in Denmark it spills over from village life into the whole country."

The queen has considerable artistic talent. She designed sets and costumes for a television adaptation of a Hans Christian Andersen story and has also illustrated Tolkien's *Lord of the Rings*, translated French and Swedish novels into Danish, and designed Danish postal stamps.

ECONOMY

DENMARK IS ONE OF THE RICHEST nations in the world, and the Danish people enjoy a high standard of living. The Danish economy is largely based on producing high-quality manufactured products. Much of what the Danes produce is exported, and Queen Margrethe herself once pointed out that Danish success is based not only on their skill in making things, but also on their ability to sell them. Because exporting is so essential to the economy, it is hoped that membership in the European Union will both protect existing markets and open new opportunities.

What makes this success so remarkable is that it has been achieved despite Denmark's extremely limited mineral resources. Denmark imports petroleum, fuels, machinery, transport equipment, metals, and paper products, so the country usually has a trade deficit. Denmark currently has one of the highest levels of debt per person among industrialized nations.

Denmark's gross national product (GNP) for 1992 was $25,930 per person, one of the highest among industrialized countries.

Opposite: **Women tend to be employed more in service professions than in industry.**

Left: **The government has started a number of schemes to support the forming of small businesses.**

FARMING AND FISHING

Although farming has become less central to the economy in recent years, 64 percent of the land is still used for agriculture, and Denmark produces three times its own food requirements. In addition, an important part of Danish industry is linked to agriculture, processing and packaging meats, dairy produce, and fish.

Danish farming is based on small family farms. Part-time labor might be employed at busy times, but statistics show that only one in six farms employ full-time help.

Ninety percent of the agricultural income comes from animal products. Danish ham, bacon, and butter are particularly popular in Britain and Germany. Principal activities are pig and dairy farming. Because of the large numbers of animals in Denmark, much of the grain and vegetables grown is used as animal feed. Barley is the most common crop and takes up around half of all farmland.

In recent years rising costs have made life difficult for small farmers, and

Small farms can still be efficient thanks largely to producer cooperatives. These help farmers by pooling capital, sharing machinery, handling marketing, and providing education on current farming methods.

the number of farms has fallen from 200,000 to less than 100,000. Those that have continued have often had to search for alternative sources of income, such as taking in tourists or renting out buildings. In 1989 legislation permitted the formation of larger farms, indicating a change in the traditional government protection of family farms.

Fishing accounts for five percent of export earnings and occupies a very small part of the work force, but it is still an important industry in many coastal towns in west Jutland. Denmark maintains around 3,000 fishing boats, and the industry employs over 10,000 workers.

Herring, eels, Norwegian pout, plaice, and cod are the most important commercial species. Ninety percent of Danish fish is exported, with fresh fish being sent daily to big European cites. There is also an important supporting industry involved in canning or freezing the fish.

Stricter limits on the size of the catch and rising costs have driven many fishermen out of business. Fishing can be a difficult and often dangerous occupation, particularly in winter, when the cold and rough seas around Denmark can turn minor accidents into life-threatening situations.

Almost all captains own their boats, and even the larger deepsea ships tend to be run by small companies that maintain just one or two vessels. The income from each trip is usually divided, half going to meet the cost of the boat, the rest being divided up among the crew.

It seems to be a national characteristic of the Danes to believe that if a job is worth doing then it should be done well. This attitude is reflected in industry, and Danish products have a reputation for combining attractive designs with first-class execution.

INDUSTRY

Among the most important Danish industrial products are electrical goods, ceramics, medical goods, textiles, and toys.

Danish industry prides itself on adapting to market demands. For example, Denmark's experience in making electrical goods has been transferred to the new growth area of high-technology computer equipment. Some of the most successful Danish computer firms are those that specialize in developing computer software for use in industry.

Much of Danish industry is either small or medium sized, with a typical firm employing a hundred people or less. There are a few larger firms, including those that make advanced machinery and chemical products. Danfoss, which produces heating and cooling devices, operates the largest factory in Denmark and employs around 12,000 people.

A LAND OF SCIENCE

Denmark has produced a number of great scientists who have played an important part in developing Danish industry as well as advancing human knowledge. The most famous Danish scientist of this century is Noble Prize winner Niels Bohr (shown at left), one of the founders of modern nuclear physics. His son, Aage Bohr, took up his work and also became a Noble Prize winner. Other notable scientists include Johannes Fibiger, who did pioneer work on treating cancer, Valdemar Poulsen, who helped invent the modern tape recorder, and Henrik Dam, who discovered vitamin K.

Today Danish scientists are particularly respected for their work in medical and technological research.

BLACK GOLD

In 1992 Denmark pumped up 7.8 million tons (7.02 million metric tons) of oil and 4.68 billion cubic yards (3.6 billion cu m) of natural gas from under the North Sea. At the present time, Denmark produces more oil and gas than it uses.

The Danish production fields are situated 125 miles west of Esbjerg. Seven rigs operate in the area, six to drill and one to act as hotel and restaurant. At any one time around 1,000 people are working offshore. Crews work for two weeks at a time and then have three weeks of leave. While on the rigs, the workers put in 12-hour days, often under harsh weather conditions.

The oilfield employs an enormous support team ranging from helicopter pilots to office personnel. In all, about 10,000 people are directly involved in Denmark's oil and gas industry.

Wind turbines are usually grouped together in windmill parks. A large park can generate enough electricity for local needs and even produce a small surplus to sell to the national network.

A LACK OF NATURAL RESOURCES

Denmark has extremely few natural mineral resources. There are deposits of limestone, clay, gravel, granite, and kaolin (a white clay used to manufacture porcelain), but Denmark stills needs to import all its raw metals and coal and until recently all of its oil. Fortunately, offshore oil fields in the North Sea have been producing petroleum since 1972 and natural gas since 1984.

There is optimism that Denmark will develop pollution-free energy sources in the future. In 1980 Denmark decided not to develop nuclear energy. Danish engineers are experimenting with other energy schemes. Future domestic energy needs may be met with biogas produced from industrial waste, bleached earth, and cattle manure.

The strong winds blowing in from the sea have enormous potential, and there are already hundreds of wind turbines scattered through the Danish countryside. The modern wind turbine is a giant propeller attached to the top of a towering metal pillar.

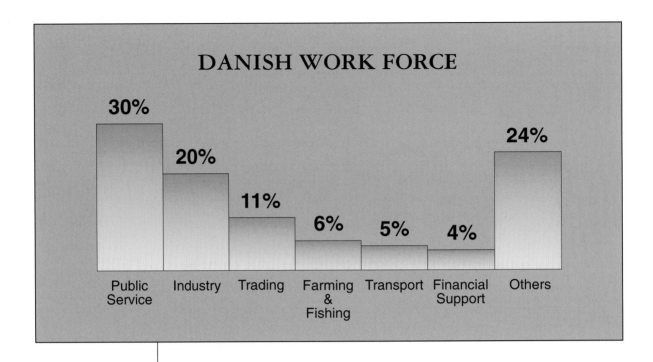

DANISH WORK FORCE

30% Public Service	
20% Industry	
11% Trading	
6% Farming & Fishing	
5% Transport	
4% Financial Support	
24% Others	

WORKING

Forty years ago nearly one in three Danes was employed in agriculture, and even 20 years ago food products were still Denmark's top export. Today agriculture employs only six percent of the work force. Instead industry and public service employ half of all Danes.

Most Danes feel that they work hard, and much of the nation's success is indeed due to the well-educated and highly skilled work force. This work ethic is established in childhood when Danish children are encouraged to find afterschool jobs, such as delivering newspapers or leaflets.

At the same time, it is very much part of the Danish culture that work should not be allowed to dominate life. The standard work week is only 37 hours, and 75 percent of Danish people work a five-day week.

Unemployment is currently (1994) at 12 percent, and for the first time, young Danes may leave the university and be unable to obtain work. At the same time, it is difficult to find people to do some of the more unpleasant manual tasks. Nonetheless, half the total population works, including 80 percent of women between ages 20 and 54.

TRANSPORTATION

The Danish transportation system is modern and efficient and can usually cope with even the worst of Danish winters. Being an island nation has posed its own special problems, and Danish engineers are now some of the most experienced bridgebuilders in the world. The latest project is a bridge and tunnel combination that will span the Great Belt to link the islands of Zealand and Fyn. There is also a future project to build a bridge or tunnel link to Sweden, although this is still in the planning stage. Despite these projects, ferries continue to play an important role in linking many of the islands and in connecting Denmark with Sweden and Norway.

The Danish railways have recently been modernized, and the number of passengers is increasing after years of decline.

Denmark has joined with Norway and Sweden to form Scandinavian Airlines System (SAS), which is one of the largest and most successful airlines in Europe. Copenhagen Airport is now Europe's fifth largest airport. There are a few small domestic airlines, such as Danair or Maersk, which can fly passengers from Copenhagen to any point in Denmark in less than an hour.

SHIPPING AND TRADE

Denmark's shipbuilding tradition stretches back to the Viking age, and today's shipyards are some of the most modern in the world. The Danish reputation for high-quality work has helped win major contracts, even in a declining market. Danish yards pioneered the idea of double-hulled oil tankers, and they are now producing a generation of advanced refrigerated cargo ships that can be operated with a crew of only six or seven.

Apart from building ships, Denmark also maintains a large merchant fleet of 600 privately owned vessels. The A.P. Moller/Maersk Group is one of the largest shipping companies in the world and owns 100 vessels.

Most Danish trade is with the European Union. The principal source of imports in 1992 was Germany, which was also the principal market for exports. Other major trading partners include Sweden and the United Kingdom.

LEGOS—ONE OF THE WORLD'S GREAT TOYS

Legos are one of Denmark's most famous exports. These interlocking building bricks are popular with children throughout the world. In fact, Lego is such a universally recognized name that many people do not even realize that it is a Danish invention.

The Lego empire was started in the 1930s by a carpenter called Ole Kirk Christiansen. During the depression there were few customers for his furniture, so Christiansen started to make sets of toy bricks out of wood. After World War II, he set up a factory to mass-produce his bricks from plastic, and they soon became one of the most popular toys in the world. It seems typical of the Danes to take an educational toy and make it such an outstanding commercial success.

At Legoland amusement park, shown here, everything is made of Legos.

DANES

THE DANES ARE A GROUP of Nordic Scandinavians who over the years have mixed relatively little with other ethnic groups. For this reason, tall, blue-eyed, blond people tend to predominate, although Danes display a full range of heights and hair colors. There are about 5.2 million Danes living in their homeland. They also form the majority of people in Greenland and the Faeroe Islands. In addition, there are large communities of Danes living around the world, including about 400,000 people of Danish descent in the United States.

Opposite: **A father and son watching a parade with flags in hand.**

Above: **The Danes are still attached to their Viking roots. These street musicians in Copenhagen are dressed in fanciful Viking costumes.**

A summary of the Danish character might include descriptions such as friendly, sociable, and talkative. They have been described as "nice and friendly, if a little boring," although U.S. writer Evelyn Waugh called them "the most exhilarating people in the world." By the standards of the Swedes and Norwegians, they are relaxed and bohemian, but their social life retains some elements of formality by English standards. They are perhaps best described as a middle-of-the-road, middle-class society. They have been brought up to keep a low profile, not to seek or gain attention by having different ideas, and definitely not to stand out in a crowd.

At the same time, Danes dislike restrictive legislation. They have a tradition of questioning authority, support for the underdog, and human rights for all. Hans Christian Andersen's fairytales are typical of the Danish humanitarian tradition: the ugly duckling becomes the swan, and the vain emperor turns out to be naked.

*Danes have great
concern for the
environment.
Public support has
enabled the
government to
bring in tough
environmental
laws. At a local
level Danes have
become some of
the world's best
recyclers. By 1990
72 percent of all
paper used in
Denmark was
recycled.*

FREEDOM AND RESPONSIBILITY

Danish people take the concept of personal freedom extremely seriously. Their country has one of the lowest crime rates in Europe, but they can be stubborn about obeying minor rules. Danish drivers seldom seem to take the speed limits seriously. Neither will the average law-abiding Dane think twice about smuggling in extra alcohol and cigarettes when they come back from vacation.

The basic belief in freedom makes Danish society tolerant toward personal relationships. People can be seen exchanging signs of affection on the street, holding hands or kissing, in a way that would bring disapproval in Europe's more conservative cultures. Swedes are often critical of the Danish behavior, and "it wouldn't happen here" is one of their favorite expressions when talking about their neighbors.

Another important characteristic of the Danish people is their concern for the world around them. Denmark is one of the few nations meeting the United Nations target of donating one percent of its gross national product to third world countries. In addition, Denmark donates large amounts of money from individuals during international disasters.

A NUMBER FOR LIFE

Every Danish person has an identity number, known as a personal number. This is used in all dealings with the government. In banks or offices a person is often asked their number before, or even instead of, their name. This rather impersonal approach seems strangely out of character to the way Danes normally act.

Personal numbers are made up of 10 digits. The first six numbers give the person's date of birth. The next four are random, but the last number identifies whether the person is female (even) or male (odd).

CHRISTIANIA

When the army closed down their former base at Christiania, a group of young people took over the old walled compound to establish a cooperative society. Twenty years later the community is still active, and in 1981 it was officially recognized as a "social experiment."

Today about a thousand people live in Christiania. The buildings are run down and in need of repair, but the walls are covered with beautiful murals and it is certainly the only area in Copenhagen where chickens run about freely in the streets!

Many of the people who have settled here are artists and those seeking a different lifestyle. They go without heating, hot water, or even a private room of their own in return for the comradeship and freedom of the community.

However, the police find it difficult to patrol the area, and other Scandinavian governments have urged Denmark to close down Christiania, which they believe is a haven for regional criminals and drug dealers. Danes are generally sympathetic toward Christiana, although you often hear comments such as, "If only they could control the criminals there."

Danish teenagers prefer casual styles, especially denim pants and jackets.

CLOTHING

Clothing in Denmark today differs very little from what you would find throughout the Western world. A lot of clothing is made in Denmark, and exclusive Danish designs sell well overseas. Blue denim is extremely popular and could even be considered the national dress of the young generation.

There is growing interest in traditional Danish clothing. For women this is a long dress with puffy sleeves worn over a white blouse. The shoulders and arms are covered, and the dresses are worn with several layers of petticoats.

Traditionally these dresses are woven at home from wool or flax. An apron in a bright checkered pattern, heavy black shoes, and a bonnet or scarf complete the outfit. There are some regional differences in bonnets, with those from Zealand being the most distinctive due to their gold and silver embroidery.

The traditional costume for men is a long jacket with tails, worn unbuttoned to show off a fancy vest beneath. Trousers consist of three-quarter length knee breeches tucked into long white socks. The shoes are made from shiny black leather with a fancy buckle, and a top hat completes the picture.

Traditional outfits might be owned by folk dancers or people going overseas who want a souvenir of their home.

Other people consider their roots to go further back, and many families have Viking outfits ready for the Viking festivals that are staged each summer. The outfit might include the famous double-horned helmet, although this is not historically accurate, as no Vikings ever wore such a headpiece.

The military have their own traditional uniforms, worn by the palace royal guard. The smart red uniforms, with their shining white cross belts and enormous bearskin hats, are brought out for ceremonial occasions.

An Ålborg folkdance group displays traditional Danish dress.

The traditional dress of leggings with built-in boots and colorful tops with high necks remain as practical as ever against the cold.

GREENLANDERS

There are about 45,000 Inuits living in Greenland. The ancestors of the Inuit emigrated there around a thousand years ago, and they consider themselves the rightful owners of the country they know as Kalaallit Nunaat—the land of Greenlanders.

Physically they are a dark, stocky people and in appearance, language, and culture have closer ties with the other Inuit people of Canada, Alaska, and Siberia than they do with the Danes. However, because of the long historic links with Denmark, there have been numerous intermarriages, and most Greenlanders can find Danish relations somewhere in their family tree. The main exceptions are communities in the east and far north, who live in greater isolation.

Traditionally the Inuit lifestyle was based on hunting sea mammals, which provided both food and furs. Hunting still plays a role in today's lifestyle, particularly for the more remote communities. The International Whaling Commission acknowledges the importance of the traditional hunting culture and allows Greenlanders to take a small number of fin and minke whales each year. Many Greenlanders are angry that campaigns by environmental groups have destroyed the market for seal furs. They argue that the Greenland seals are not endangered and that

Greenlanders often
choose bright
colors in their
clothing or in
painting their
houses. This is a
contrast to the
long, dark and
snowy winters.

A LOST TRADITION

The Greenland Inuits traditionally lived in closely knit communities. Large communal houses, shared activity, and hardship brought them together; they looked after each other in hard times and shared their resources. Today the move to individual houses and separate jobs has drastically changed their lives. The community feeling that was essential to their lifestyle is being lost.

sealing is the only economic activity available to some isolated communities.

Today it is largely the older people who make a living from small-scale hunting and fishing. They still use dogsleds, although the traditional kayak has largely been replaced by modern boats. Young Greenlanders are likely to seek work in one of the shrimp or fish processing factories or to go off to university in Denmark.

Like many traditional societies, the Inuit face problems adapting to a changing world. Unemployment and alcoholism—one helping to cause the other—are major concerns. People are starting to realize how important it is for the Inuit to have pride in their culture, so many towns have established museums to preserve the memory of the old lifestyle.

There is also an active campaign to save the Greenlandic language. Danish is the common language of business, education, and administration, but local newspapers and radio use both Danish and Greenlandic. There are a growing number of books published in Greenlandic, and television programs are increasingly being broadcast with Greenlandic subtitles.

Greenlanders have distinctive Mongoloid features. Their ancestors migrated to North America from Asia.

49

FAEROESE

The Faeroe Islanders have the automatic right to live and work in Denmark. It is an offer that few people from this close-knit community have taken, although many Faeroese go to Denmark to study.

The Faeroese descend from Norwegian settlers who replaced an Irish settlement in 800. For several hundred years, the Faeroes were part of Norway. When the union between Norway and Denmark ended in 1814, the Faeroe Islands remained with Denmark. In 1948, after much debate

The Faeroese, descendents of Norwegian settlers, have features similar to Danes.

about independence from Denmark, the Faeroes were granted home rule.

Today the population is around 45,000, distributed in densely populated settlements varying widely in size. There are about 100 towns and villages, of which the largest is Tórshavn with 15,000 inhabitants. The two smallest islands have only a single family each. More than one-third of the population resides on Streymoy, the main island.

Houses are made of wood, with a deep basement in concrete and a metal roof, although the traditional turf roof is also returning to favor. In the villages family and friends may help a young person build his or her own house. Homes in Tórshavn are expensive.

A quarter of the Faeroe Island workforce make their living from fishing or fish processing. The Islands support around 260 large fishing boats and over a thousand smaller craft. Since the land is rugged, only six percent is under cultivation, while the rest is used for grazing sheep.

Although unemployment is low, the choice of jobs is limited, and workers must be flexible both in trade and location. Since there is no unemployment compensation, workers are often obliged to change professions in order to find work.

Wages are higher at sea than on land, but people in fishing have a working day of 12-18 hours seven days a week, and their work is physically demanding as well as dangerous. If they fish in remote areas, they may be away from home for up to five months at a time.

Faeroe Islanders are extremely proud of their history and culture. They have a rich legacy of storytelling and folk songs, and these tiny islands continue to produce award-winning writers. Another important part of the Faeroe's cultural heritage are the folk dances and the music that accompanies them. These are mostly chain dances where partners are exchanged around the circle.

This century has seen a growing movement to preserve the Faeroese language, which once was in danger of being replaced by Danish. Today Faeroese is taught in schools, and most Faeroese speak both Faeroese and Danish.

THE DANISH SENSE OF HUMOR

Danes pride themselves on their sense of humor and are always willing to laugh and joke with each other. A great deal of Danish humor involves people laughing at their own mistakes and characteristics.

New Year's Eve and the first day of April are two days when playing practical jokes becomes almost a national sport. Even the big newspapers join in with the April Fool's Day fun, and there is usually some front page story reporting on a fictitious event.

A popular form of humor, particularly at summer festivals, consists of live cabaret shows that parody famous people. Politicians are frequent targets, but even the royal family does not escape. The same kind of humor is also featured in magazines and on television.

THE GERMAN MINORITY

The largest minority living in Denmark is a group of people from Southern Jutland who can trace their origins back to Germany. This community has lived in Denmark for many generations, and there are few if any racial tensions or problems. A handful of towns with the largest German minorities offer schools based on the more rigid German system. German churches also attract a larger congregation than their Danish counterparts. Other cultural differences, for example a fondness for different foods, have tended to dissolve in recent years.

People of Danish background living within the German-influenced areas are often more openly patriotic than other Danes. The most obvious sign is the number of Danish flags flying in gardens. Their neighbors are unable to respond to such teasing, as it is illegal to rise the German flag on Danish soil.

NEW IMMIGRANTS

Until recently Denmark has been a largely homogeneous country, with few new arrivals. Now a growing number of immigrants are seeking to settle, attracted by Denmark's healthy economy and tolerant social attitudes. By January 1992 there were 170,000 immigrants in Denmark. It has been estimated that approximately five percent of the 5.2 million inhabitants are of immediate foreign descent. The majority of these come from other Scandinavian countries and blend unnoticed into the local community.

Turks form the largest non-Scandinavian group in Denmark and number around 32,000 people. The last 10 years have seen an increase in the number of arrivals from Iran, Sri Lanka, Africa, and the former Yugoslavia. Many immigrants have built up successful small-scale businesses, particularly shops and restaurants.

Immigration is now becoming an important political issue. As social tensions increase, Queen Margrethe has used her New Year address to remind Danes of their reputation for racial tolerance.

Denmark has a particular responsibility to immigrants from Greenland. Greenlanders often come to Denmark to study, and many find it difficult to adapt to Danish life. Peter Hoeg's book *Smilla's Sense of Snow* made many Danes realize that the problem is partly the result of two different cultures failing to understand each other.

A student in an Ålborg kindergarten, one of the growing number of Danish immigrants.

LIFESTYLE

THE DANISH PEOPLE ENJOY ONE OF THE HIGHEST standards of living in the world, and the strong state welfare system is a major influence on the Danish lifestyle.

Denmark was one of the first countries to introduce state social welfare schemes. Health care and education are available to all Danish people free of charge. There are generous unemployment benefits and retraining schemes for those who are out of work. If Danes are sick, the government pays them 90 percent of their weekly wage. When people retire, they collect a state pension and social services, and nursing homes are available.

Whatever their income all Danish people receive a yearly "children's check" of around $900 for each child in the family.

The success of this state welfare system is proven by statistics. The infant mortality figures are seven in 1,000, a record beaten only by Japan and Liechtenstein. The literacy rate in Denmark is 99 percent and the average Danish man can expect to live until he is 72, the average woman until she is 78.

Opposite: **A shopping street in Copenhagen attracts a crowd of Danes.**

Above: **Spectators enjoy a puppet show at Legoland.**

Providing such service is expensive, and on the average Danes pay between 30 percent and 40 percent of their salary in taxes. Many people complain about the high level of taxation, which is becoming an increasingly important political issue. Over the next few years, Denmark must also face up to the problem of how a shrinking work force can continue to support a growing number of elderly people.

TWO DIFFERENT LIFESTYLES

The weather is probably the single major influence on the Danish lifestyle, and it sometimes seems that the whole nation changes character with the seasons.

Bicycling is a favorite summer activity.

In summer, Danes take every opportunity to be outdoors in the sunshine. Favorite activities include walking, cycling, jogging, or sailing. Other people are content just to head for the nearest park to sit and relax. With the warm weather visitors flock to the popular Tivoli Gardens in Copenhagen, tour boats cruise the waterways, and restaurants start putting their tables outside on the pavement.

During the summer months every small town promotes weekly festivals and outdoor concerts. Providing it does not rain, such events usually attract hundreds of spectators.

With the arrival of the cold, dark winters, social life moves indoors. People rush away from work to seek the warmth and comfort of their homes, and evenings are spent enjoying leisurely meals with friends and relations. It is time for candlelight and open fires—the season to create that important feeling of hygge.

Winter also has its own fashion. Danish cardigans are expensive and extremely popular. Because of sympathy toward the Greenlandic hunters, there has generally not been as strong an anti-fur movement as in other places, so fur clothing is fairly common.

RURAL AND URBAN LIFE

Although 84 percent of the population live in cities, even urban Danes retain their love of the land. Many urban residents go to rural cottages for summer vacations. "Colony gardens" are also popular; these are rented plots of land near the city where people can grow flowers, fruit, and vegetables or maintain a small greenhouse. City dwellers often use them for weekend retreats.

Probably the main difference between rural and urban Danes is the close sense of community that has survived in many villages. In the village community, people are far more likely to know their neighbors by name, they seem to have more time to stop and talk when they meet in the street, and they are more likely to be there to help out when somebody has problems. City dwellers live a more rushed life.

A traditional method of roofing a house.

Fifty-seven out of every 100 Danes own their own property, and 10 out of every 100 have a second holiday cottage in the countryside.

Virtually all the new ideas and theories about giving birth have been published in Denmark, and each has won its share of converts. Probably the most important trend has been the growing number of Danish fathers now present at the birth of their children.

BIRTH

For several years the birth rate in Denmark was low and people were predicting the population would begin to decline. Instead the 1990s brought a slight reversal of this trend, although most families today only have one or two children. During the development of the modern health-care program, most births took place in hospitals. This pattern is now being reversed, with a growing number of women electing to have their babies at home, with a doctor or midwife in attendance. This is more for economic rather than social reasons. Four or five days in a hospital were once quite normal after giving birth. Now the health care system is starting to cut costs, and most mothers are sent home within 24 hours of the birth. As a result, women seem less enthusiastic about going to the hospital.

After the birth it is usual for the mother to be given flowers, and friends and relatives bring gifts for the baby. It is highly unusual to give gifts before the baby is born. The old practice of blue gifts for boys and pink for girls seems to be returning to fashion.

Mothers are entitled to four weeks of maternity leave before the baby is born and 24 weeks afterward. Fathers are entitled to two weeks of leave after the baby is born. In addition, the last nine weeks of maternity leave can be transferred to the father.

BIRTHDAYS AND GROWING UP

Danes make a big fuss about birthdays. On the morning of their birthday, people are expected to stay in bed pretending to be asleep. Sometime before breakfast, the rest of the family will burst in on them bringing their presents and cards. They are likely to carry small Danish flags and sing the two popular Danish birthday songs. The most famous one describes events that will happen on the day and has a chorus of *"hurra, hurra,*

hurra." If it is a school day, children might bring hot chocolate and cookies for their classmates.

It is usual for children to be given a birthday party. Here the guests will be treated to special foods including a cake-man, which, as the name suggests, is a cake baked in the shape of a man. Hot chocolate is another favorite on these occasions. Children also play party games, such as Pin-the-Tail-on-the-Donkey.

The 18th birthday is considered the start of adulthood. This is the age when young people can vote and drive cars. It is usual to celebrate the day with a big party. When boys pass the age of 18, they may have to complete a year of national service in the armed forces. Not all Danes are called up, and a draw is made to see who will have to go. Young Danes trained in certain professions, such as teaching or medicine, might opt to do two years of volunteer service overseas instead of military training.

Danish children on an excursion.

59

Denmark has invested a great deal of money in its school system and the standards are generally very high. Materials are plentiful and the number of children in each class is often as low as 20.

Although the government gives some guidelines as to what should be taught, teachers enjoy considerable freedom in preparing lessons they think are best suited to their own class.

EDUCATION

School is compulsory in Denmark from the ages of 7 to 16 years. Many children also spend a year in preschool. Although there are private schools, the majority of Danish children attend the government-run *folkeskole* ("FOLK-es-skoh-la"). These schools combine elementary and junior high school education in one building.

Danish schools operate in pupil groups, with the same classmates staying together throughout their school life. Each pupil group is assigned to a teacher who stays with them throughout their time at the folkeskole. As the children become older, they have lessons with other teachers, but they still retain close contact with their original teacher.

It is common for pupils to address teachers by their first names, and the relationship is often close enough for children to phone the teacher at home when they have problems. In addition to parents coming to school for open days, schools are experimenting with teachers making visits to

ADULT EDUCATION

Denmark has led the way for the rest of the world in the area of adult education. Adult education is considered an important part of the Danish culture, and many Danes continue their education with evening classes or summer courses.

These courses are organized by the local authorities, who provide financial support and make school buildings available during the evenings. Subjects offered might be educational, such as history or foreign languages; recreational, such as art or photography; or vocational, such as computer studies or automobile repair.

N.F.S. Grundtvig founded the first folk high school in 1844. His idea of offering further education to adults for their personal development has been copied in the United States, England, and Canada. There are now about 80 folk high schools in Denmark, all of them residential. Courses are often sponsored by educational and commercial organizations in order to provide training or to generate interest in a particular field, especially arts or social science subjects. Those who attend courses may be following a particular interest or laying the foundation for a change of jobs.

the children's homes so they can learn more about the family.

After the ninth grade, when the children are 15, they take the leaving examination. Those who do well in this exam usually elect to go to gymnasium, a secondary school that offers three-year courses leading to university study. Those who are not ready to go to gymnasium after the ninth grade might stay in school for an extra year. At the end of this they can take a second exam, the advanced leaving examination. There is still the chance of going to gymnasium at the end of the 10th year. Other students typically enter technical school.

The Danes take education seriously.

There are five universities in Denmark. Copenhagen University was founded in 1479. It has over 26,000 students and a teaching staff of 1,500. Århus University provides education for about 14,000 students and has about 800 full-time teachers and many part-time teachers. Odense University provides education not only in traditioal academic subjects but also in music, business, social studies, and teacher training. In addition, there are numerous technical colleges and specialized training institutions.

THE ROLE OF WOMEN

Women make up a large part of the Danish work force. Statistics show that there are 86 women working for every 100 men. This high percentage has been possible thanks to the state-supported system of childcare. In 1990, 71 percent of children between ages 3 and 6 were in daycare.

However, there are still some inequalities in the workplace. Women do not hold an equal share of the high-level positions. Neither are they as well

Women's lives in the next generation will be considerably different from those of their mothers.

TO SMOKE OR NOT TO SMOKE?

Smoking has become a major issue in Denmark over the last five years, with big campaigns to persuade Danes to give up tobacco. It is too early to tell how successful this will be, but figures for the past 10 years show only a minor decline in the number of cigarettes being consumed. At the same time there has been an increase in pipe smoking.

One area no campaign looks likely to challenge is the habit many older Danish women have of smoking small cigars.

represented in industry as they are in service areas such as education and health. Although by law women must be paid the same as men for doing the same work, in practice this is sometimes difficult to enforce.

With so many women working, Danish men usually play a major part in bringing up children. Yet it would be wrong to presume that the domestic roles have reached total equality. A recent magazine survey revealed that the average Danish man still does less around the house than his wife, even when both are working. In addition, when they do take on household chores, Danish men generally prefer less demanding tasks such as washing dishes.

One area where Danish women have exerted a particularly strong influence is politics. They acquired the vote in 1915, five years before women in the United States, and today women hold around a third of the seats in parliament. When a recent government came to power, it appointed eight women ministers. The popular former Minister of Education, Ritt Bjerregaard, has not been afraid to express her views, particularly in matters of foreign policy, where she is considered a leading expert. She has been a strong advocate of the European Union.

Women are a particularly powerful force in referendums. It is widely believed that it was the vote of Danish women that played the decisive part in initially defeating the Maastricht Treaty.

Large families are unusual in Denmark.

MARRIAGE

Danes display a more relaxed attitude toward marriage than people from other European nations. It is not at all unusual for young people to live together or even start a family without being married. As many as 200,000 people have chosen to live in "paperless marriages." These are couples who have accepted all the responsibilities of being together and who are recognized as being a couple by their friends but have not gone through any religious or civil ceremony.

It is hoped that by living together first young people will see if their relationship looks likely to last before committing themselves to marriage. That is the theory, but there seems to be little evidence of it actually working, because divorce is very high in Denmark. About 30,000 Danish couples get married each year, and around 15,000 get divorced.

Although marriage is no longer considered socially necessary, most

A Danish couple with their child.

couples do eventually elect to make a formal commitment to each other. However, Danes now tend to be older when they marry. Typically a man is around 33 years of age and a woman 30.

There are both civil and church weddings in Denmark. A civil wedding usually takes place at the town hall and is performed by the mayor or his deputy.

A church wedding is generally more traditional and elaborate than a civil service. Typically the bride wears a long white dress, and the groom arrives at church in a formal tuxedo or at least a smart suit. The groom selects one close friend to act as "best man." The bride is escorted into the church by her father or a close male relation, but it would be unusual for her to have bridesmaids. The exception might be if there are close female relations who are still very young.

As the couple leaves the church, friends throw confetti, and it is not unusual for the waiting guests to wave tiny Danish flags.

Women in Denmark may keep their maiden name, and husbands may take their wife's name if they choose. Children may bear either parent's surname.

65

THE IMPORTANCE OF THE HOME

It would be quite unusual to find a Danish house without a flag pole in the front yard. Danish people raise the flag on national holidays, if somebody in the house has a birthday, or just because it is a bright, sunny day.

Unlike neighboring nations such as Great Britain and Germany, where pubs, clubs and beer cellars have traditionally been important social centers, Danish social life has always centered on the home.

Certainly most Danes are extremely "house proud" and take great care and pride in their homes. Houses are large by European standards, and in the typical family 30 percent of the income goes directly to furnishing and running the house. This includes heavy heating bills during the winter.

There has been a major building program since the war, and many Danes live in houses that are less than 50 years old. The government has subsidized construction of new houses and offers maintenance grants to improve older properties. Low-income families may also qualify for a rent subsidy. The result is that slum or substandard housing hardly exists in Denmark. Instead the pattern repeated in every Danish town is of rows of neat, individual houses, with clean streets and well-kept gardens.

HOUSING

Housing is not cheap in Denmark. Typical prices in a small town might be:

A small apartment........$78,000
A modern detached house with small garden.......$93,000
A chalet type house with garden........ $120,000
A larger house on the edge of town with a big garden..... $171,000

As a result of high prices, many newly married couples start life in an apartment, perhaps rented from the government. Despite close family ties, it is very unusual for young Danish couples to move into the home of a another family member. Many people who work in Copenhagen or other cities choose to live in surrounding villages and commute to work.

SENIOR CITIZENS

Danish people receive a pension at 67 years of age and there are now schemes to help them retire earlier. After 60, most Danes can elect to take redundancy, which means they can stop working but still receive a percentage of their salary until they qualify for their pension.

As people get older, help is provided to allow them to stay in their own homes for as long as possible. When people get too old to manage alone, they are usually given a place in a nursing home.

Most Danish senior citizens continue to lead active lives.

RELIGION

THERE ARE NO RECENT SURVEYS of religious beliefs, but it is believed that between 92 and 97 percent of Danes belong to the state-supported National Church of Denmark, which is Evangelical Lutheran.

The Danish parliament has control over the church, but it does not interfere with religious practices. Unlike many other European countries, the Danish church has no supreme spiritual leader. Church affairs are managed by 10 bishops.

Few Danes attend church regularly, and except at Christmas and Easter, there is seldom a full congregation. Similarly, it is quite unusual to hear Danes talk about religion, which is considered an area of private concern of little interest to other people. Rural and fishing communities, particularly in Jutland, tend to support the church more than urban populations.

Opposite: **The distinctive style of country churches in Denmark is seen in Nyker Church in Bornholm.**

Below: **A minister presides over the Queen Mother's birthday preparations.**

The only person in the whole of Denmark who does not enjoy religious freedom is the reigning monarch, who must be a member of the state church.

Bishop Absalon was a powerful figure who established schools, churches, and monasteries throughout the country.

HISTORY OF THE CHURCH IN DENMARK

The credit for converting the Danes to Christianity goes to the French monk Ansgar, known as the Apostle of the North. With the support of King Harald Bluetooth the Roman Catholic faith was able to establish a strong following. In the 10th and 11th centuries over 2,000 rural churches were built in Denmark. The king may have been influenced by political advantages when he adopted the new religion. One of the great fears at the time was that the powerful Christian kingdoms to the south would try to invade Denmark.

Over the next three hundred years, the Roman Catholic Church grew into a rich and politically powerful force. It owned many estates and farms and received a percentage of all the grain grown in the country. At the same time, the church upset many ordinary people by allowing members of the Danish nobility to become religious officials, often simply to increase their own wealth. As a result, support grew for the Protestant faith. King Frederick I, although staying loyal to the Catholic Church, invited Lutheran preachers to visit Denmark. As a result, it was this branch of the Protestant religion that emerged as the most popular.

The ongoing feud between Protestants and Catholics turned into civil war when King Frederick died in 1533. His elder son, Christian, favored the Protestant religion, whereas the younger brother, Hans, was a Catholic. After three years of fighting, the Protestants prevailed. Once in power, King Christian III quickly appointed new bishops and converted Denmark to the Lutheran religion.

THE VIKING GODS

The Vikings had their own religious beliefs that are still familiar to us today, although we now call them myths and legends.

The Vikings believed the gods lived in a land called Asgard. In Asgard was the Great Hall of Valhalla, where dead warriors passed the time fighting all day and feasting all night while they waited for the last great battle at the end of time. People inhabited the middle world, which was surrounded by a great uncrossable ocean. On the third level lay Nifheim, the icy world of the dead.

Odin was considered the king of the gods. He was the god of battle, but he was also a poet and able to foresee the future.

His son, Thor, is the best known of the Viking gods. With his magical hammer, Mjollnir, he kept the troublesome giants at bay and wrestled with the great sea serpent that surrounded the middle world. Thor was visualized as a redbearded man of immense size, always dependable and trustworthy, although he could lose his temper quickly and was often slow to grasp the important points of an issue.

Other gods included Freyr, god of plenty, Njord, god of the seas, and the heroic Tyr.

All our knowledge of the Viking gods comes from a small collection of documents, and these were not written down until the 13th century. Therefore our knowledge is neither complete nor undisputed. For example, historians question the relationship of Odin and Thor. Odin has always been considered the king of the Viking gods, yet it is Thor who gets more mentions on runic stones. It is possible that the Vikings actually considered Thor to be the more important god and that later writers overemphasized the importance of Odin.

Vikings often wore a small replica of Thor's hammer, such as the one shown here, for protection from danger. Later, the molds used to make these were converted to make crosses for the new Christians.

The most important sources of information on Viking mythology are two collections of poems by Icelandic writers known as the Edda Poems.

KIERKEGAARD AND GRUNDTVIG

Two religious thinkers of the 19th century have had a profound influence on the way Danes think about religion: N.F.S. Grundtvig and Søren Kierkegaard.

N.F.S. Grundtvig (1783–1872) was responsible for a religious revival that became the major influence on the Danish church from 1848 on. He believed that Christianity is not based on right beliefs, religious experiences, or morality, but rather on the sacraments. The word of God is to be found in the rites of baptism and communion, and in the Lord's Prayer. Grundtvig expressed his view of Christianity in his hymns, for which he is still admired.

Søren Kierkegaard (1813–1855) emphasized the choice everyone must make between God and the world. He argued that there are no logical reasons why one should choose one or the other; instead people must decide for themselves whether to make the "leap of faith" to believe in God. Anyone who asks for rational explanations or proofs is trying to get around the necessity of making a personal decision. Kierkegaard is known today as the father of existentialism in philosophy.

Danish churches frequently have a model of an ancient ship hanging from the ceiling, a token of the importance of the sea to this seafaring people.

EVERYDAY INVOLVEMENT

Unless Danes make an objection in writing, a small percentage of their taxes are automatically paid to the church. Few Danes opt out of this contribution, as most people wish to have church support at times of marriage, births, and deaths. About half the people getting married in Denmark choose to do so in church, and around 80 percent of Danish people have their children baptized.

A large number of Danes have their children confirmed. Confirmation usually takes place when children reach their early teens, and they are expected to attend six months of special classes. A successful confirmation is usually rewarded with gifts and is seen as an important step toward adulthood.

CHURCH ARCHITECTURE

Many of the churches in Denmark are 800 or 900 years old. These simple buildings give the Danish countryside much of its character. They were generally built on hilltops out of whitewashed stone, and many have medieval frescoes on the walls and ceiling. The favorite theme is a warning about the punishments facing those who live corrupt lives.

The most important cathedral in Denmark is the one at Roskilde. Bishop Absalon started the cathedral in 1170, but it was 300 years before it was finished. Extensions have been added right up to the present day. It is a large brick building and from the outside has little of the charm of the great cathedrals of France or Germany. Yet, inside the cathedral, one finds a museum of Danish history. Over 30 Danish monarchs are buried within the church, and the priceless artwork includes a statue by Bertel Thorvaldsen, one of the leading sculptors of the 19th century. A famous feature of the church is the 16th-century clock that on the hour sends out a figure of Saint George to slay the dragon.

Modern Danish church architecture is best represented by the Grundtvig Church in Copenhagen. Building started in 1921 and was not finished until 1940. Although it is a giant, cathedral-sized structure, its unique design is inspired by Danish country churches. The facade recalls the shape of an organ, a tribute to the hundreds of hymns Grundtvig composed.

The Grundtvig Church was designed as a tribute to N.F.S. Gruntvig, who was the most important influence on the contemporary Danish church.

THE CHURCH COMMUNITY

Churches in Denmark are often very active within their communities. In addition to their religious duties, vicars carry out considerable social work. A great deal of effort goes into attracting children to the church; in addition to confirmation classes, many churches run their own youth clubs. Women are fully accepted and make up over 10 percent of the nation's clergy.

On Sunday, services are broadcast over the radio for those unable to come to church. Many Danes prefer to listen to these broadcasts in their own home rather than attending a public church service.

Whitewashed churches dot the Danish countryside.

MANY RELIGIONS

There is complete freedom of religion in Denmark. The Roman Catholic Church is the largest minority, with around 28,000 people.

There is also a small but long-established Jewish community. In physical appearance Danish Jews are almost indistinguishable from the rest of the population. A few orthodox men might stand out by wearing the traditional skullcap. As people in Denmark do not generally display strong feelings about religion, the Jewish minority have little trouble integrating into their local community. There might be minor conflicts at a family level when there are marriages between Jews and Christians, although even here Danish tolerance and belief in an individual's freedom of choice is likely to prevail.

Other Christian groups include the Swedish Church, the Russian Orthodox Church, and the Reform Church.

The arrival of recent immigrants has resulted in a growing number of Muslims living in Denmark.

These Somali women are some of the many recent Muslim immigrants to Denmark.

LANGUAGE

DANISH IS SPOKEN BY about six million people in Denmark, the Faeroe Islands, and Greenland. When Danish is written, it is a single, formal language, although in the spoken form it has several dialects.

Danish is closely related to Swedish and Norwegian. In fact, Danes and Norwegians can usually understand each other if they speak slowly and clearly. When written, these two languages are even more similar, since they share a large vocabulary but differ in pronunciation. Swedish, although still closely related to Danish, has sufficient differences to make it very difficult for Danes and Swedes to communicate.

Opposite and above: **Denmark's small size and its crossroads location has led Danes to become familiar with several languages. One frequently finds foreign languages alongside Danish in signs and publications.**

The predominant language on Greenland is Greenlandic, which is closely related to languages spoken by the Inuit of Northern Canada, Alaska, and Siberia. Because few of the resident Danes learn Greenlandic, Danish is widely used in teaching, administration, and business. Many young people also understand English.

The Faeroe Islanders speak Faeroese, a Scandinavian language closely related to Icelandic and Norwegian. In the 16th century, Faeroese fell into disuse as a written language but survived as a vehicle for a rich oral literature, including sagas and poems sung to folk dances. In the mid-19th century, a written Faeroese language was created, but it was not until 1937 that it was used in the schools and 1948 in legal institutions. There is a vital literature in Faeroese, and eight newspapers are published in the language.

HISTORY

About 4,000 years ago, the early settlers of Scandinavia still spoke the same language as the tribes living farther south in Germany. Over many hundreds of years the language spoken in Scandinavia slowly changed until it became quite different from the Germanic language it had started out as. All the basic words still came from the old German language, but there were now so many words borrowed from Greek and Latin that a new, Scandinavian, language had emerged.

By the 12th century Danish started to diverge from the language spoken in Sweden. At this time Denmark ruled Norway and so had considerable influence over the people there. This is one reason why the Danish and Norwegian languages are still so similar today.

The earliest manuscripts appeared during the 14th century. Most of these recorded local laws but are particularly important to students of language because they show that there were various written dialects used in different parts of Denmark.

King Harald ordered a runic stone to be placed at Jelling with the words, "King Harald had these memorials done in honor of Gorm his father and Thyra his mother, the Harald who won all Denmark and Norway and made the Danes Christians."
This famous stone has been called the baptismal certificate of Denmark and marks the start of the written history of the country.

The Jelling Stone contains an inscription on one side and a design on the other.

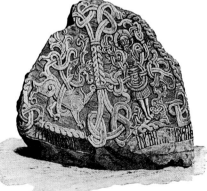

THE INFLUENCE OF DANISH

The Viking expansion resulted in a number of Scandinavian-speaking settlements that left their mark on their neighbors. Iceland and the Faeroe Islands continue to speak a dialect of Scandinavian today. Colonies in the Hebrides, the Isle of Man, Ireland, the Danelaw in England, and Normandy in France stopped speaking Scandinavian after a short time, while the Shetlands continued until 1750 and the Orkneys and Scottish coasts until about 1700.

The Danish colonization of the Danelaw has resulted in many Scandinavian words being incorporated in English. For example, *law, by-law, fellow, skull, skin, sky, window, birth*, and *thrift* all come from Scandinavian.

The first evidence of writing in Denmark dates from A.D. 200. These first inscriptions used the ancient runic alphabet and were carved onto stones or wooden boards. At first there were 24 runic letters, but by 900 only 16 letters were still in common use.

When printed books started to appear at the end of the 15th century, it became important to have a common version of the written language. It was the dialect used in Copenhagen, the seat of government, that became recognized as standard Danish. Another important influence was the first translation of the Bible, because the grammar and spelling used in the translation became the standard.

It wasn't until the 18th century that modern rules of grammar started to be accepted in the way they are used today. Spelling took even longer to develop into the standard modern form, but in 1889 the government finally adopted spelling rules to be used nationwide.

In modern times Danish has borrowed words from other sources, particularly from French, German, and English. Most musical and banking terms derive from Italian, the bulk of the cooking and women's fashion terms from French, a large number of maritime words from Dutch, and scientific terminology chiefly from the classical languages. Words are borrowed to describe technical or scientific terms that do not exist in Danish. We see this clearly demonstrated in computer language. Danes use the term *hard disk* because there is no direct translation. However, when computer manuals talk about memory they use *hukommelse*, the Danish word for memory.

DIALECTS

Although written Danish was largely standardized by the start of this century, numerous versions of the spoken language still existed, particularly in rural communities. Today there are three main dialects, those of West Jutland, the central islands, and Bornholm. The Jutland dialect differs the most from the rest of Denmark. People from Jutland who have a heavy accent might even have some problem making themselves understood in Copenhagen. Under the influence of radio and television, the dialects are dying out, replaced by a standard Danish. This educated Danish is called *rigsdansk* ("RIJ-dansk"), but in its pure form is only spoken by television presenters and a few people from the middle classes. The vast majority of Danes speak a version of rigsdansk influenced by their regional accent.

THE ALPHABET

Danish has three extra letters compared to the Roman alphabet.

An ordinary *a* is pronounced as the *a* in the word *bar*, but *å* sounds like the *a* in *paw*.

The letter *æ* makes the same sound as the *e* in *egg*.

The special *ø* is pronounced like the *u* in *turn*.

In addition some of the other letters of the alphabet are not pronounced the same way they would be in English. The letter *j* is pronounced as the English *y*, and *w* as *v*.

The *ø* and *å* letters have only been written in this form for the last 40 years. Before this, the *ø* was written as *oe* and the *å* as *aa*. Some Danish people still insist on using the old version, particularly with place names. Ålborg, for example, can often be found written as Aalborg.

A sign showing the Danish letter ø.

COUNTING IN DANISH

0	*nul* ("nool")	6	*seks* ("sehks")
1	*en* ("et")	7	*syv* ("SEE-oo")
2	*to* ("toh")	8	*ottle* ("AW-der")
3	*tre* ("tray")	9	*ni* ("nee")
4	*fire* ("FEE-rer")	10	*ti* ("tee")
5	*fem* ("fehm")		

Danish names larger numbers in a way similar to French, which becomes quite complex if one stops to think about their meaning. Seventy, for example, is *halvfjends* ("HALF-ee-as"), which literally means three times 20 plus half of 20.

Copenhagen's National Library houses an excellent collection of books in various languages.

Many words are borrowed from English, notably in sports and journalism, but also names of products, fabrics, and social and political terms.

THE IMPORTANCE OF A SECOND LANGUAGE

English-speaking travelers in Denmark get so used to Danish people being able to understand them that they are often surprised when they finally meet a Dane who does not speak good English.

Learning another language is very important to Danes. Businesspeople need to speak English when dealing with overseas customers, and students in higher education need to refer to studies and books written in English. It is estimated that 57 percent of the general population and 97 percent of university graduates speak English. In public libraries Danish and English books are mixed together on the shelves.

Because Germany is both a close neighbor and an important trading partner, many Danes also learn German. In the areas where Jutland borders Germany, most Danes are able to communicate in German.

DANISH NAMES

Twenty-one percent of the population of Denmark share the three surnames of Jensen, Nielsen, and Hansen. In fact, two-thirds of all Danish people have a surname that ends in *sen,* including the Pedersens, Larsens, Andersens, Christensens, and Petersens.

Fashions in given names have changed over the last few years. Traditional Danish given names frequently borrow saints' names. Names such as Kirsten and Mariam for girls and Peter, Hans, or Søren for boys have now lost much of their old popularity. Mette and Sofif are now extremely popular names for young girls, with Anders, Thomas, Jakob, and Kasper becoming increasingly common for boys.

There is also a trend for people to give their children more original names, such as Pi or Pil. Rebecca, seldom used in Denmark until the last 10 years, has become popular. It is also common, particularly with girls, to join two names together, as in Anne-Mette or Anne-Louise.

Two names that look likely to survive any changing fashion are the royal names of Christian and Frederik, which remain as popular as ever.

The Danes tend to be informal. The formal mode of address "De" has more or less been abolished. Inherited and social titles are not taken very seriously, but earned titles, such as doctor and master and titles indicating a person's position in business or government, are generally used.

Probably the most used word in the Danish language is *tak* ("tahk"). It can mean "thank you," "please," or "excuse me," and sometimes seems to be added to every sentence you hear!

ARTS

THE EARLIEST KNOWN HUMAN IMAGES found in Denmark were carved on a 10,000-year-old aurochs bone, but it was during the Viking period that a distinctive culture emerged. The Viking period saw great developments in the arts. Carpenters, blacksmiths, and other crafts workers excelled, producing finely decorated weapons, drinking horns, musical instruments, and jewelry.

The first Danish instrument was the *lur* ("luhr"), a long, curving, horn-shaped instrument that produced a hoarse, sonorous, trumpet-like sound. Many of these beautiful instruments have been found in Viking graves.

The skilled decoration on weapons, tools, and ornaments indicates ancient traditions of art and metalworking. Viking design is characterized by animal ornamentation consisting of ingeniously intertwined animals.

The Viking period also produced the first written records of Danish history, which were carved in runes onto large stones or wooden boards. The true runic period was 900–1050, but there are inscriptions of various kinds from several hundred years before and 200 years after.

The Viking period is described in the *Gesta Danorum* by Saxo Grammaticus. Written in Latin around 1200, its 16 books range from legendary history to chronicles of the author's own time. A defender of royalty, Saxo promotes the virtues of loyalty, moderation, and courage.

Opposite: **A statue of the Little Mermaid sits in Copenhagen harbor.**

Above: **A craftsperson working on the famous Royal Copenhagen pottery.**

85

One of Denmark's most important contributions to literature has no connection with Danish writers at all. William Shakespeare set Hamlet *in Kronborg Castle, just north of Copenhagen. It tells the story of a Danish prince and was clearly inspired by an old Danish folk legend.*
The story of Hamlet is told in the Gesta Danorum.

WRITERS

Ludvig Holberg is known for his many comedies, as well as histories and essays. His liberal humanism has been of lasting importance to Danish culture. His works advocate relativism and tolerance, practical common sense coupled with social reponsibility. Hans Christian Andersen and Søren Kierkegaard dominated the 19th century.

More recently, Martin Andersen Nexø won international fame with his book *Pelle the Conqueror,* which portrayed the humble people of his native Bornholm. Johannes Jensen was inspired by the doctrine of evolution in his short prose pieces, novels, and lyrics. He was awarded the Nobel Prize in literature in 1944. Karen Blixen, who wrote under the name of Isak Dinesen, was known for her *Seven Gothic Tales* and her memoirs of life in Africa, *Out of Africa.*

Peter Hoeg is the best known of the contemporary writers. His latest book, *Smilla's Sense of Snow,* examines the way Greenlanders are treated in Denmark, and shows that Denmark's social services can seem very impersonal and harsh.

HANS CHRISTIAN ANDERSEN

Hans Christian Andersen is unarguably Denmark's most famous son. Andersen was born to a poor family in Odense in 1805. His father was a shoemaker, and his mother wanted Hans to find a similar trade, perhaps as a tailor. Andersen, however, was convinced he was destined to become famous and, at the age of 14, set out to Copenhagen to seek his fortune as an actor and singer. The young man did have a fine voice, but after several years in the capital he had still not found employment in the theater. Instead Andersen started to write, and when he was 24 he published a collection of stories and then a play. Neither was a great success, and Andersen left Denmark to travel around Europe. While in Italy he wrote a novel called *The Improvisatore*. Although set in Rome, this was in fact the story of Andersen's own childhood. The book became popular in Denmark and was soon published in England and Germany.

Andersen had already been working on a collection of four fairy stories, and these were published a few weeks after his novel. The book was badly printed on poor paper and was not well received by the critics. Fortunately, a few close friends encouraged Andersen to continue writing his fairy stories, and from then on he brought out a new volume every Christmas. Included in these little booklets were *The Little Mermaid*, *The Ugly Duckling*, and *The Emperor's New Clothes*, stories that made Andersen famous around the world. His fairy tales have been translated into more than 100 languages.

Andersen never married and lived in furnished rooms or hotels all his life. He was an avid traveler, making 29 journeys in Europe. His childhood home in Odense is now a museum.

Andersen's fairy tales, based on a belief in living miracles, combine a complex sense of humor that exposes pettiness and egoism with a firm belief in eternal justice. His writing shows extraordinary sensitivity and subtlety, but these qualities tend, unfortunately, to be lost in translations.

Jazz players entertain on a canal boat in Copenhagen.

MUSIC

Danes enjoy all types of music, ranging from classical to pop.

There are 10 professional orchestras in Denmark, the most important being the Royal Danish Orchestra and the Danish Radio Symphony. Many of the musicians who play in these orchestras were trained at the Royal Danish Conservatory. The best known of all Denmark's classical musicians is the composer Carl Nielsen.

Jazz has a particularly strong following in Denmark, and each year Copenhagen puts on a major festival with over 400 concerts. In addition to top international artists, local bands perform free in the city's parks and restaurants. This active scene has made Copenhagen a favorite city with many young American jazz players.

DANISH POP MUSIC

There is a lively Danish pop scene, although this is heavily influenced by fashions and trends in the United States and Britain. Danish pop stars perform in Danish or English, and are quite likely to switch languages with each song.

The most famous of Denmark's pop artists is Kim Larsens, now a veteran of many years in the business, but still as outrageous as ever. Of the popular new acts, Dr. Baker and a four man rock band called TV2 have built up a strong following.

CARL NIELSEN

Carl Nielsen was born in a little village south of Odense in 1865, near the birthplace of Hans Christian Andersen. Like Andersen, he was from a poor family and left for Copenhagen to seek his fortune. And like Andersen, he was successful. At the banquet for his 60th birthday, Nielsen told the audience that his mother had always said to him, "Don't forget that Hans Christian Andersen was poor like you." With Andersen's inspiration, Nielsen was to become a composer of international stature.

From his musical father, Nielsen learned the music of Hayden and Mozart as well as the traditional airs of his native Fyn Island, and he incorporated both in his many musical compositions. After studying at the Copenhagen Conservatory, he joined the Royal Orchestra as a violinist and eventually became its conductor. He later taught at the Conservatory and became its director shortly before his death.

During his long career, he wrote six symphonies, two operas, many choral works, a variety of concertos, piano compositions, and quartets, an organ work, and many songs and ballads.

The folk high schools encouraged development of the popular Danish song in the 19th and 20th centuries.

89

PAINTING AND SCULPTURE

Danish painting has a distinctiveness that sets it apart from European painting in general. It is characterized by a quiet intimacy, combined with a deep love of and respect for nature, and an always apparent, instinctive dislike of extremes and heroics. A distaste for sentimentality and vulgar emotional display is evident in the tone of restrained simplicity.

Modern art in Denmark traces its roots to the early part of the 19th century. The most important figure of this period is C.W. Eckersberg, who is considered the father of Danish painting. Like most artists of his day Eckersberg made a grand tour, living and painting in Paris and Rome, where he learned a strictly objective, penetrating, almost microscopic

Young painters always find it difficult to sell their early work, but there are good opportunities in Denmark for artists to find a market. Museums and town councils have yearly grants to purchase art work, while many large firms have established funds to build up their own private collections.
There are also special grants to allow established artists to add murals or statues to public buildings.

A modern sculpture stands at an intersection in Fyn.

BERTEL THORVALDSEN

Bertel Thorvaldsen is the only Danish visual artist to have achieved worldwide fame. The son of an Icelandic woodcarver who had settled in Denmark, he was born in Copenhagen and studied at the Copenhagen Academy, where he won a scholarship to Rome. He found success with his statue *Jason* when he was still a student in Rome, staying there for 40 years. His restrained classicism earned him an international reputation as the foremost sculptor of his time and he had one of the most spectacularly successful careers of the 19th century. His return to Copenhagen in 1838 was regarded as a national event in Danish history.

Thorvaldsen excluded dramatic expression from his work in order to achieve an ideal beauty. Although his works were once regarded as the perfect reincarnation of classical art, they now seem somewhat cold.

study of nature. Eckersberg then returned to Denmark, where he spent 35 years teaching at the Royal Academy of Art in Copenhagen.

The generation of artists trained by Eckersberg created the Golden Period of Danish painting. Christen Købke is one of the best known painters of this age; when one of his paintings recently came on the market, the National Gallery in London purchased it for over $390,000.

The 19th century is dominated by the sculptor Bertel Thorvaldsen, who achieved international fame during his lifetime. Today there is a museum in Copenhagen dedicated to Thorvaldsen's work.

Erik Frandsen is one of the most respected artists of the present generation. His work ranges from a swirling blue mass of colors to paintings such as *Portrait of Ester*, in which automobile tires are incorporated into the picture to give it three dimensions. Lars Norgard, with thought-provoking works such as *Mod lyset*, and Claus Carstensen, who often works with foam, are among today's other top artists.

The Louisiana Museum in North Zealand has one of the leading collections of modern art in Europe.

Danish sculptors continue to produce some of the country's most exciting and original pieces, with Robert Jacobsen leading the way with his unique iron sculptures.

The little town of Skagen on the very tip of north Jutland has always held a special place with Danish artists who are attracted there by the solitude, the beauty of the area, and the special light. Skagen artists are naturally inspired to produce scenes of sea and sky, and some of their best work can be seen in the local museum.

Postal stamps proudly display Danish design.

DESIGN

Danish designers are renowned for making household objects interesting and attractive as well as functional. This appreciation of good design is very much a part of Danish culture, and it has been said that every Danish home is a miniature modern art museum. Danish furniture, lamps, silverware, pottery, toys, and fabrics often win international design awards.

Foremost among designers is Hans Wegner, who, with his famous furniture, has been described as the founder of modern Danish design. Other key figures include Kay Bojesen, who is best known for his tableware, pottery master Christian Poulsen, and Poul Henningsen, whose modern lamps set the standard for a whole generation of young designers.

Danish porcelain is particularly famous, with the Royal Copenhagen, the Hilland Glass Factory, and the Bing and Grondahl Factory producing some of the world's finest serving porcelain and decorative china.

The Royal Copenhagen reputation was originally built around one dinner service. In the 1780s King Frederik ordered a 1,800-piece service as a gift for Catherine II of Russia. Each piece was handmade and decorated with paintings of Danish plants and flowers, and the set took 15 years to make. The Empress died before the gift was completed, and so the set was never sent to Russia. This one project established the international reputation of both the Royal Copenhagen Company and the whole of the Danish porcelain industry. Since then, Denmark has had a reputation for producing fine porcelain.

ARCHITECTURE

The Danish gift for design is reflected in the work of the nation's architects. The Planetarium in Copenhagen, with its unique cylindrical shape, is one of the finest examples of modern Danish architecture.

Professor Arne Jacobsen is considered the first of the great modern architects. Several of his buildings, including the SAS Hotel and the Danish Central Bank, are important Copenhagen landmarks.

Many of the top Danish architects have produced their finest work overseas. Danish architects designed the Parliament Building in Kuwait and the Foreign Ministry in Saudi Arabia. Arne Jacobsen went to England to design the new St. Catherine's College in Oxford.

It was another Dane, Jørgen Utzon, who created one of the most remarkable buildings of the century when he designed the Sydney Opera House.

Jørgen Utzon designed the Sydney Opera House in Sydney, Australia, considered a masterpiece of modern architecture.

DANCE, DRAMA, THEATER

The Copenhagen Royal Theater in the center of Copenhagen is home to the state ballet, theater, and opera companies. Of these the Royal Danish Ballet Company has built up the highest international reputation. During the 1830s the great French director August Bournonville settled in Denmark, and under his inspiration the company established a magnificent repertoire of dances. The Royal Danish Ballet Company still performs many of these classical dances today but complements them with an exciting program of original modern ballets. This versatility is one reason the company is so admired. They have been invited to dance in theaters around the world, including in the United States, Japan, and China.

In 1988 the Royal Ballet held a dance festival at which the first Hans Christian Andersen Ballet Awards were presented. It is hoped that these awards will become the ballet version of the Oscar.

Copenhagen supports between 8 and 10 theaters, and there are also permanent theaters in most provincial cities. Smaller towns are visited by traveling troupes, and one Danish drama group turned an old barge into a floating theater!

Theater offers limited opportunities for modern Danish writers, many of whom also write for television. The government sponsors Danish theater by subsidizing theatergoers' organizations. These in turn make tickets available to the public at reduced prices.

A unique part of the amateur drama scene consists of Viking plays. These often involve two or three hundred local people who work with a professional director to reenact scenes from Viking legends.

The Copenhagen Royal Theater is home to the state ballet, theater, and opera companies.

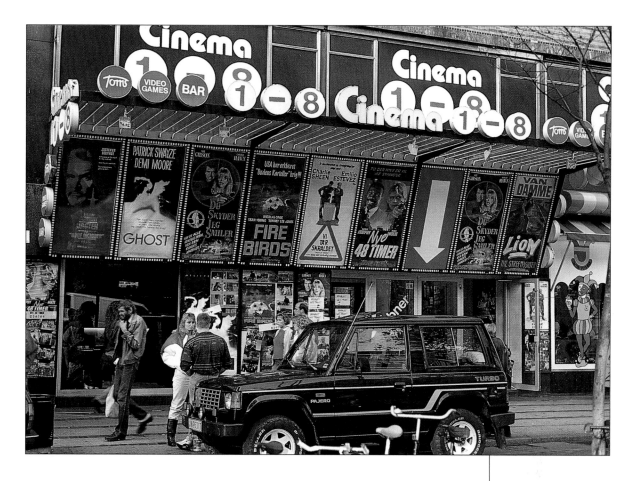

FILM

At the turn of the century, during the age of the silent movie, the Danish film industry became notorious for tackling daring subjects, often with a sexual theme. Apart from being provocative, Danish movies could also be beautiful. Carl Th. Dreyer's *La Passion de Jeanne d'Arc* is considered one of the best silent movies ever made. With the arrival of the talking picture Danish films became restricted to a local audience.

Today Denmark produces between 10 and 16 major movies each year. Recently the industry has received recognition with two Oscars in the Best Foreign Film category. The first came in 1988 for Gabriel Axel's *Babette's Feast*, based on a Karen Blixen short story, the second the following year for Bille August's *Pelle the Conqueror*.

A multi-screen cinema in Copenhagen shows Hollywood movies as well as Danish productions.

LEISURE

MOST PEOPLE IN DENMARK WORK a five-day week, leaving the weekends free. In addition, the long summer days allow ample time to participate in outdoor activities during the evenings. Danish people generally make use of this free time to enjoy a variety of hobbies and sports.

A nation that spends so much of the winter in the cold and dark is particularly anxious to get outdoors as soon as the warmer weather arrives. Therefore sailing and cycling have always been popular. Recently more and more Danes have followed the international trend and become avid joggers. There are fun runs every weekend, and the Copenhagen marathon now attracts 4,000 runners.

The Danish countryside, with its endless walking and riding trails, is another source of relaxation. Trails are well maintained and marked, and there are many local walking societies that offer organized hikes.

The winter brings its own activities. The Danes are avid skaters. On weekends many people simply enjoy walking through the frosty countryside. Chess and bridge are popular games.

Most people enjoy five weeks of vacation a year, and each summer thousands of Danes fly south to the beaches of Italy and Spain. Denmark was one of the first countries to pioneer the idea of "package vacations." It is also quite common for Danish people to take several months off work, usually just after finishing their studies, to travel to more distant parts of the world.

Opposite: **Organized bicycle races are popular with many Danes.**

Below: **The Roskilde Music Festival draws thousands of spectators.**

A COMMITMENT TO SPORTS

Organized sports were introduced by British residents. The oldest athletic club in Denmark was founded in 1892. Four years later Denmark was one of a handful of nations represented at the first modern Olympic Games.

Although soccer is the most popular sport, badminton has brought Denmark the most international success. Flemming Delfs and Lene Koppen were winners of the men's and women's titles at the first world championship in 1977. The rise of Asian players has prevented Denmark from winning further world titles, but they still rank as one of the strongest nations in Europe.

Speedway, where motorbikes are raced around a narrow cinder track, is another sport Denmark has excelled at. Hans Nielsen, with 19 world titles (including nine team titles), is the most successful speedway racer of all time. Jan Pedersen was world champion in 1991, and many of Denmark's riders compete in the British professional league.

SOCCER, THE NATIONAL GAME

Denmark was one of the first countries in the world to take the British game of soccer seriously, and by the turn of the century the Danish team was considered the best on mainland Europe. However, once the larger European nations started to organize professional leagues Denmark could no longer compete. It wasn't until the late 1980s that Denmark once again built up a strong national team. The main reason for their recent success is that all the best Danish players now play for professional clubs in Germany, Italy, or Britain.

Denmark won silver medals at the 1988 European Championships and played well in the World Cup two years later. By 1992 many of their best players had retired, and Denmark did not even qualify for the finals of the next European Championships. When the Danish team was invited to replace Yugoslavia, who had withdrawn, the Danes amazed everybody by beating Germany 2–0 in the final. This was Denmark's first victory in a major soccer championship.

Soccer quickly became the national game, and it remains the most popular sport today, with around 300,000 registered players of all ages.

Thousands of Danes made the short journey to Sweden for the final game in 1992 and demonstrated their pride by waving flags and painting their faces in the red and white Danish colors.

BICYCLING

Bicycling is a favorite family activity on summer weekends. Because Denmark is a flat country with beautiful scenery, it is ideal for cycling. And when the weather is nice, a bicycle tour is a pleasant way to get out and see the scenery.

As well as being a pleasant form of recreation, bicycling is also a major means of transportation in Denmark. Many families have bicycles, and cycling is considered both good exercise and a way to help the environment. Even in Copenhagen, bicycles can be seen everywhere, and they are often the best means of transportation.

Denmark's country lanes are quiet and peaceful, and most major roads have parallel bicycle tracks. Within towns and cities there are elaborate systems of bicycle paths, often with their own stoplights and road signs. Automobiles are required to give way to bicycles.

There are specially marked cars on the trains for storing bicycles, and bicycle parking lots are found everywhere. Another interesting Danish idea is the coin-operated air pump found outside many stores.

PAUL ELVSTROM, OLYMPIC YACHTSMAN

Paul Elvstrom is probably the greatest Olympic yacht racer of all time, and he won four consecutive gold medals in the Finn class. His Olympic debut came at the 1948 games in London where he failed to finish in the first race of the series. He didn't panic, and a string of high places over the rest of the week secured his first gold medal. In 1952 and 1960 Elvstrom was so far ahead of the other competitors that he did not even need to turn out for the last race of the series.

Yachts in Copenhagen. Many families keep a small boat to sail for their own enjoyment.

WATER SPORTS

The Danes traditionally have a special love for the sea, and sailing draws enormous numbers of enthusiasts. Yachting has the strongest following in North Zealand, where many of the best natural harbors are situated.

Denmark's enthusiasm for sailing, rowing, and cycling has helped win a steady flow of Olympic medals. This total has now passed 150, a record better than many larger countries. Denmark has also produced several Olympic sailing champions. The most famous is Paul Elvstrom, a legend in Denmark and winner of four Olympic medals.

The classic domestic race is the Round Zealand Regatta, which attracts 2,000 boats every year. The contesting boats gather opposite Kronborg Castle for the start. The race lasts between two and three days and covers 220 nautical miles.

Other water sports make use of Denmark's many lakes and fjords. Rowing and canoeing are popular and many young Danes are now turning just as enthusiastically to windsurfing.

Fishing, in either fresh or salt water, has a large following, with Jutland being the favorite location.

TELEVISION

It would be unusual to find a Danish house without a television. In fact watching television is the nation's favorite pastime; about 40 percent of people's leisure time is spent this way. There are two national channels. Channel One is run by the government and does not allow advertising. Channel Two operates with a combination of government sponsorship and advertising.

The Danes make some of their own programs, usually small-scale productions, such as quiz games or travel features. They buy other shows from the United States, Germany, or Britain and translate them into Danish, so programs such as *The Cosby Show* are familiar to Danish people. Depending on what part of the country people live in, it is usually possible to tune in to either Swedish or German television. There are also regional stations that provide local news.

TILTING THE RING

A favorite sport in South Jutland is the equestrian event of tilting the ring. Events are staged in different towns throughout the summer months and draw many enthusiastic competitors and hundreds of spectators.

Riders use a long pole like a medieval lance to hook rings suspended above the ground. There are 24 rings, each slightly smaller as the riders pass down the course.

Tilting is a colorful event, with riders dressed in their best equestrian clothes.

TIVOLI GARDENS

Tivoli, in the center of Copenhagen, is one of the symbols of Denmark. It covers only two or three blocks, but within this space there are 25 amusements, 28 restaurants, theaters, bandstands, concert halls, and a museum.

Many Copenhagen residents buy a season ticket and visit the Gardens several times each week. Around four million visitors pass through the gates each year during the four summer months when Tivoli is open.

Tivoli had its 150th anniversary in 1993; to celebrate the event an 89-foot-long replica of a sailing ship was placed in the central lake and made into a floating restaurant.

Theme parks are growing increasingly popular in Denmark. One of the most interesting is Legoland in central Jutland. Here one can wander around scale models of the most famous buildings of Denmark or view a 20-meter-high version of Mount Rushmore, all constructed out of plastic toy bricks.

CHESS

The Danes have been chess players for many centuries. There are stories of Viking kings playing the game while resting between raids, and chess pieces have been found in remains from the Viking period.

The most famous international competitor is Bent Larsen, who gained the title of grand master at the age of 21. In 1967 he set a world record by winning six international tournaments in succession.

FESTIVALS

DANES ENJOY SEVEN NATIONAL HOLIDAYS a year, most of which celebrate religious occasions. Christmas is by far the most important of the holidays.

There are also numerous festivals and cultural events that are held annually. Many of these create a great deal of excitement within a local area, or even nationally. Some sporting events, particularly the biggest yacht races, are also colorful festivals with their own traditions.

In addition to annual events, special celebrations are staged on important historical anniversaries.

NATIONAL HOLIDAYS FOR 1995:

January 2	New Year's Day
April 14–17	Easter
May 12	General Prayer Day
May 25	Ascension Day
June 5	Constitution Day
June 5	Whit Monday
December 25–26	Christmas Holiday

Important Annual Events:
Queen's Birthday
Copenhagen Carnival
Round Fyn Yacht Race
Round Zealand Yacht Race
Midsummer's Night
Frederikssund Viking Festival
Copenhagen Jazz Festival
Arhus Jazz Festival
Hans Christian Andersen Festival

Opposite: **The Ring-riderfest traditionally begins with a parade.**

Traditional dancing at a local festival in County Rentmeester.

SPECIAL DAYS IN DANISH CULTURE

There are several holidays that are specially related to Danish culture.

Midsummer is a tradition dating back to Viking times. Bonfires are an important part of the day, a tradition that recalls the burning of witches many centuries ago. Today a life-sized model of a witch made by stuffing old clothes full of paper or rags is placed on top of the fire. Midsummer is a favorite time for a family barbecue.

Fastelvn ("fasta-laon") takes place on February 21, before the fasting leading up to Easter begins. Nowadays it is considered a holiday for children. A special fastelvn event is a game called "beating a cat out of the barrel." In this game a wooden barrel full of gifts is hung from a tree, and children line up to hit it with sticks. Once it breaks, the presents cascade down and are divided up. The barrel game has a cruel history, for long ago a cat would have been placed inside, and the barrel hit until the poor creature was dead.

Fastelvn is also a day for children to wear fancy dress costumes. These often reflect favorites from the latest movies, such Ninja Turtles or Batman.

On the **Queen's Birthday** residents of Copenhagen, particularly children and the elderly, gather outside the palace. The queen traditionally comes onto the balcony just before midday to say a few words to the crowd. In return she is greeted with nine cheers.

Constitution Day is on June 5 and celebrates the adopting of the new constitution in 1849. It is usually a half-day holiday and is a particularly important day for politicians, who are kept busy with numerous political speeches and meetings.

Another historic celebration is **Liberation Eve** on May 4. This commemorates the end of the German occupation in 1945. On this night Danes place a lighted candle in their windows. Liberation Eve generally means more to older people, who still remember the war years.

The **Copenhagen Carnival** takes place in May and was originally a religious festival, although the religious importance has been more or less forgotten. The celebrations are scattered around different neighborhoods, with street parties and many people putting on fancy dress costumes.

Lunchtime at an agricultural show in Fyn.

Participants at the Santa Claus World Congress in Copenhagen.

CHRISTMAS

The first sign of Christmas arriving is lights and decorations going up in the center of town. Shops add their own Christmas window displays.

The evening of December 23, sometimes called "little Christmas eve," is the traditional time for families to decorate their homes with a Christmas tree hung with lights, stars, hearts, tiny Danish flags, and Christmas figures.

Much of this would be familiar to visitors from the United States, but candles play a more important role in the Danish decorations than they do in other cultures. The *Nisse* ("NISS-ah") also add a special Danish touch to the celebration.

For children Christmas eve is the most important day of the celebration because this is when they receive their presents. The early evening starts with carols around the tree. One of the adults is likely to disappear for a few moments to dress up in a red cloak and white beard because it is traditional in Denmark for children to receive their presents direct from Santa Claus.

There is a special dinner on Christmas eve. The meal starts with a special rice pudding called *ris ala a mante* ("rihs-ALAH-man-tah"). One whole almond is placed in the mixture, and there is a special gift put aside for whoever finds it. The main course is goose, duck, or crispy pork. Pork was once eaten only by families who could not afford anything better, but now it has become a Christmas eve favorite.

Christmas day is often quieter and more for the adults. Many families

THE DANISH *NISSE*

The *Nisse* are dwarflike creatures who have been part of Danish folklore since pagan times. Traditionally the *Nisse* are portrayed as little old men with gray beards. They were originally farm dwellers who lived in the barns and outhouses. Although everybody knew the *Nisse* were there, they were never seen, expect perhaps for a fleeting glance out of the corner of the eye. As long as nobody  upset them, the *Nisse* usually did no harm but lived side by side with the human occupants.

In the last hundred years, these half-feared spirits of the farmyard have become increasingly associated with Christmas. The once shy *Nisse* now seems happy to appear in the middle of store displays, on Christmas cards, or to be part of the decorations in homes. The *Nisse* has changed his image as a result of his new role, and is now shown as a young, clean shaven, elf-like figure.

Nisse have become so much a part of the Christmas holiday that few people associate them with any other time of year.

attend a church service in the morning, even if they do not go to church at other times of the year. Children spend the day visiting friends and playing with their new Christmas gifts. Christmas dinner, served early in the afternoon, is likely to be a buffet with all the family's favorite foods.

NEW YEAR'S

At around 6:00 p.m. on the last day of the old year, the queen appears on television to give her New Year speech. This is an important event for Danes, and most try to watch the yearly message.

On New Year's eve children are allowed, even expected, to engage in a few naughty but harmless tricks. An old favorite was to push firecrackers through mailboxes, although this is now discouraged as being too dangerous. The family flagpole remains a likely target for New Year tricks, and many parents wake up in the morning to find a chair or the old Christmas tree suspended from the top of the pole.

Demonstrating the traditional art of lacemaking at the Kniple Festival in Tønder.

EASTER

The religious importance of Easter has faded, but the holiday is still important in Denmark as a celebration marking the end of the long, dark winter and the start of spring.

The actual holidays are Maundy Thursday, Good Friday, Easter Sunday, and Easter Monday. This long holiday makes it possible for families to visit relatives or friends who live in other parts of Denmark. Adults exchange gifts of flowers, particularly tulips and daffodils. Daffodils are in fact sometimes referred to as Easter lilies. Children receive gifts of chocolate Easter eggs, the hollow insides filled with a collection of sweets.

Young Danish children are told the story of the Easter Rabbit who comes into the garden to hide eggs for them. Many Danish parents hide chocolate eggs all over the garden, and seeing the children hunt for them is part of the holiday fun. If the weather interferes, the game can be moved indoors.

Families wishing to follow a traditional celebration make eggs an important part of the holiday meals. Hardboiled eggs start the day for breakfast, and children spend hours coloring and decorating the shells. "Soiled eggs," which are hardboiled eggs in mustard sauce, are eaten later in the day. Lamb is usually the main Easter meal.

An agricultural show cow parade draws some lovely contestants in Fyn.

CARNIVALS

The summer months are busy with festivals and carnivals. Agricultural shows remain important events, as the Danes have never forgotten their farming past. Besides parades of prize farm animals, agricultural shows also attract numerous craft stalls. Each June Roskilde stages the biggest agricultural show in northern Europe, with over 2,000 animals on parade.

Special antique fairs also attract large crowds, as do horse fairs and craft shows.

Most towns have their own special carnival day with a street parade, fun fair, and cultural events. For towns by the sea, the carnival often centers around the harbor. The anniversary of a city's founding or a famous person's birthday inspires special celebrations, with parades, sporting events, exhibitions, concerts, plays, and guided tours. Not only are such events a way for Danish people to enjoy themselves, but they are good for tourism and local commerce. Odense stages a famous Hans Christian Andersen festival each year that attracts visitors from all over the world.

Rejsegilde ("RAI-se-gildehr") is a special ceremony that takes place when a new house has been raised, and a wreath of green and red ribbons is ceremoniously placed on the framework of the roof for good luck.

111

FOOD

MOST DANISH PEOPLE like to get home early from work to enjoy a long evening with their family. As a result, breakfast and lunch are often eaten quickly with little fuss. The evening meal, in contrast, is an important occasion for the family to spend time together.

The Danish are particularly fond of herring, pork, soup, meatballs, and above all, the sandwiches known as *smørrebrød* ("SMEHR-brehrth").

The Danes say that "meals are for being together, not just for filling up!" The appearance of the table, the atmosphere in the room, and above all the company will be just as important in making a meal a success as the food itself.

It is polite in Denmark to begin eating as soon as the meal is ready and not to let it get cold while waiting for late guests to arrive or for a television show to end. Guests are always encouraged to take second portions.

Opposite: **An open-air produce market in Roskilde town square.**

Left: **A bread shop window display of various breads and sandwiches.**

A traditional meal centered around meat- balls and potatoes.

TYPICAL MEALS

Bread is a major part of breakfast. Rye bread is very popular for both breakfast and lunch. Alternatively, people might eat *rundstykker* ("rond-STOO-kehr"), which are crusty rolls, or *kryddere* ("KROH-dor"), which are cold, toasted rolls. These are all known as *morgenbrød* ("MORG-brohd"), or morning breads, and are likely to be served with cheese, jam, and perhaps eggs. When the family wants a more filling breakfast, they might add cold meats and fish to the table, and pastries are often served on weekends.

Breakfast cereals have also become popular. Coffee, tea, juices, and milk are the most likely breakfast drinks. Porridge was once the traditional Danish breakfast, and quite a few Danes still find this an agreeable way to start the day. Although Danish bacon is a popular breakfast food around the world, that is certainly not the case in Denmark.

The most typical lunch consists of open sandwiches known as smørrebrød. These are either packed at home or bought fresh from the special smørrebrød shops that can be found in every neighborhood. Children frequently take smørrebrød for their school lunch. If the family is having lunch at home it is quite common to include a hot smørrebrød.

A popular alternative to smørrebrød is a hamburger from a fast food stall. Although international fast food chains are establishing a market in Denmark, they have strong competition from local brands. Small hamburger stands can be found in every town square, specializing in the high-quality Danish style of hamburger.

In summer people often take their lunch down to the park or city square and enjoy a little extra time in the sunshine.

After school, children are given a small snack with milk. The main meal is eaten about 6:00 p.m. when all the family has arrived home. Popular dishes for the main meal include pork tenderloin, hamburgers, meatballs, herring, or cold table.

Danish hamburgers are called *hamburgerryg* ("ham-bohr-urg") and are made from high quality pork. Meatballs, known as *frikadeller* ("FRAHK-ah-dilehr"), are a very common Danish dish, and there are numerous local recipes, such as the South Jutland meatballs that have smoked bacon added. Fish is also quite popular in this fishing country, especially herring.

As dinner is often eaten early, it is usual for Danish families to end the day with a light supper of coffee, cakes, pastry, or a small *smørrebrød* selection.

As one would expect from a nation with so much dairy produce, Denmark has produced a wonderful range of cheeses. The most famous is Danish Blue, which is quite distinctive with its blue veins and powerful taste. Other cheeses special to Denmark include Samsoe, Havarti, and Estrom.

COLD TABLE

The cold table is a very popular way of eating in Denmark and is particularly useful when unexpected guests arrive. Usually the host prepares and serves one or two warm dishes. The rest of the meal is a buffet of cold meats, vegetables, salads, cheese, and sweets. There is a selection of breads, often served heavily buttered, and herring is a favorite appetizer.

It is important to have supply of fresh plates on hand so as not to mix the different tastes, and a good host quietly keeps all the serving plates filled.

A selection of smørrebrod is served on a wooden board.

THE ART OF MAKING GOOD SMØRREBRØD

If there is one food that Denmark is famous for, it is smørrebrød. These are open sandwiches, each one designed to be a little meal in itself.

Smørrebrød require a firm bread with a crisp crust. Although several types of bread are used, dark rye bread is by far the favorite. Getting the right size is important. Cutting the bread bigger than 2x4 inches will spoil the compact effect.

Using the correct butter is considered equally important. Smørrebrød literally means buttered bread, and the butter should be evenly spread without missing the edges. Butter has several jobs to perform. It is a flavoring, it stops the bread from getting soggy, and it acts as a paste to hold the toppings in place.

The list of toppings is endless, but favorites include roast beef, cheese, eel, egg, herring pate, plaice, salami, salmon, tongue, and shrimps. A typical heated smørrebrød would be cooked ham with egg, fried liver with onion and bacon, or fried pork with onion.

A garnish should be added, both to bring out the taste and to be attractive to the eye; however, only one or at most two garnishes should be added to each individual sandwich.

A selection of smørrebrød is served together on a wooden board, but care is taken to keep the strong flavors at one end. When eating smørrebrød, it is polite to take only one of the little open sandwiches at a time.

DESSERTS

Most Danes enjoy rounding off a meal with a sweet dessert. Marzipan ring cakes, a nut-filled coffee cake called *kringle ("KRING-el")*, and layer cake are all popular.

Fruit jellies known as *rødgrød ("REHR-grebr")* are another favorite desert; they are usually made from fresh fruits and homemade jelly. Depending on the season, *rødgrød* might be served with raspberries, black currants, strawberries, or rhubarb. Danes prepare an apple cake flavored with almonds and lemons and topped with thick cream.

Denmark is known for its excellent cheeses.

Danish pastries—rich, flaky, sweet rolls—are famous all over the world. They are generally eaten with breakfast or as a snack.

SONDERJYDSKE FRIKADELLER (SOUTH JUTLAND MEATBALLS)

8 oz (224 gm) cooked meat
4 oz (112 gm) smoked bacon
1 sliced onion

2 slices white bread
2 eggs
pepper, salt, butter

Cut the bread into small squares and soak in water. Mince the meat, bacon, and onions together. Squeeze out the bread and add to the mixture. Add two beaten eggs. Season with salt and pepper and shape into meatballs. Fry slowly in butter until brown on all sides. Serve with potatoes and vegetables or wait until cold and cut into slices to place on brown bread.

Having drinks at a streetside cafe is a popular way to spend an afternoon.

Beer is expensive because the two main breweries tax beer to support social causes. Drinkers can support the arts by drinking Carlsberg or the sciences by drinking Tuborg.

DRINKS

The two drinks that best capture the spirit of Denmark are coffee and beer.

Danes are great coffee drinkers, and most people expect their coffee to come from freshly ground beans. Milk is usually added, and perhaps sugar, depending on the individual's taste. Coffee is the most likely drink for breakfast and morning and afternoon breaks. Children are generally not encouraged to drink coffee but are more likely to drink tea or milk.

Denmark is also famous for making beer, and the Danes as a nation drink a great deal of what they produce. Some people even joke that drinking beer is part of their Viking legacy. According to one legend, the cry of *skål* ("skohl") comes from Viking times when warriors drank from the skulls of their dead opponents after a battle!

However, the Danish fondness for beer probably has its roots in the 16th and 17th centuries, when everybody drank a weak beer because so much of the country's water supply was unsafe. Today the most popular beer is a light lager, served very cold.

Snaps ("shnaps") is another traditional Danish drink. It is quite different from the German *schnapps*; Danish *snaps* is an alcoholic drink made from potato or barley and flavored with caraway or other herbs. It is served ice cold and drunk quickly, not sipped. You would not expect to drink *snaps* with hot food, but it is common for adults to have a *snaps* with cold snacks of herring or cheese.

DRINKING IN DENMARK

People are now starting to question the amount of beer being drunk in Denmark. What particularly worries and embarrasses many people is the amount of beer drunk in public. It is not unusual for people at work to share a case of beer during their breaks, or for a group of people to quite nonchalantly drink from bottles as they stroll down the streets.

Although there is some pressure to change this image, the strong Danish belief in individual freedom makes it difficult to enforce restrictions. Nonetheless, some firms are now banning alcohol during work time, and a few public areas have become alcohol-free zones.

Danes joke that the only word of their language recognized throughout the word is the drinking toast skål. *This ritual way of toasting friends and guests is an important part of Danish culture.*

SKÅL

When people gather together around the table, no one starts drinking until the host or hostess has officially welcomed everybody. To do so they lift their glass, make eye contact with the guests, and say *skål* ("skohl"). This toast is then repeated by everybody at the table, with everyone raising and lowering their glasses together. There is then a third, less formal round of toasts, after which people are free to start the meal.

An Ålborg fish shop shows an impressive array of fresh fish.

INFLUENCES ON DANISH FOOD

The modern Danish diet has been influenced by trends and events that can be traced back several hundred years.

At the very heart of modern Danish cuisine is the tradition of farmhouse cooking with its large helpings. One example of this farmhouse influence is the popularity of soup. Even today, with the availability of modern convenience foods, many Danish people still prefer to make their own homemade soups. In doing so people are using recipes developed many years ago to take advantage of ingredients that were plentiful on Danish farms, such as chicken, oxtail, and vegetables. Danish soups often have small dumplings, meatballs, or vegetables floating in them.

Denmark's long tradition as a fishing nation also influences the modern diet. Herring holds a special place in Danish cooking and is eaten at just about any time of day.

As more Danes travel overseas, the Danish diet is becoming increasingly internationalized. It is now far more likely for a Danish family to cook spaghetti at home, go to an Indian restaurant for a meal, or drink a bottle of wine with their meal.

SPECIAL CARE IN SETTING THE TABLE

Danish china, table linen, and tableware are among the finest in the world, and most homes have a varied collection of table settings for creating different atmospheres. Danish people are likely to decorate the table for most evening meals and not just on special occasions.

In a country where the seasons affect the lifestyle so much, flowers play a special role as table decorations. In addition to those bought at the florist, wildflowers and grasses are picked during the summer. In autumn dried flowers bring the browns and golds of the season into the room, and even in the dark months after Christmas a tiny display of snowdrops or crocuses often brightens the table.

Candles are also used to add light and warmth to the room and contribute to the special *hygge* atmosphere.

THE DANISH KITCHEN

The Danish kitchen is a very important part of the house and brings out the best in Danish design. Real estate agents attempting to sell a house often use pictures of the kitchen to attract buyers. A typical Danish feature is to have an open design where the kitchen and dining room are separated only by a low wall.

DENMARK

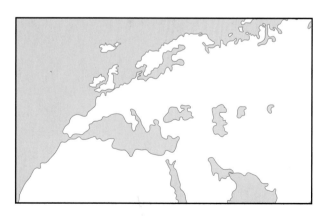

QUICK NOTES

OFFICIAL NAME
Kingdom of Denmark

CAPITAL
Copenhagen

FORM OF GOVERNMENT
Constitutional monarchy

PRESENT GOVERNMENT
A coalition of Social Democratic Party, Center Democrats, Radical Liberals, and Christian People's Party. Elected February 1994.

CURRENT PRIME MINISTER
Poul Nyrup Rasmussen

COMMUNICATION
43,614 miles (70,174 km) of roads. 1,535 miles (2,470 km) of railways.

LANGUAGE
Danish, with small minorities speaking Faeroese, Greenlandic, and German. English widely spoken as a second language.

CURRENCY
100 öre to one krone. Krone converts at approximately six for one U.S. dollar.

POPULATION
5,180,614 (1993 estimate)

AVERAGE NUMBER OF CHILDREN PER FAMILY
1.7

LAND AREA
16,639 sq mi (43,094 sq km)

HIGHEST POINT
Yding Skovhøj, 568 ft (173 m)

COUNTIES
Århus, Bornholm, Copenhagen, Frederiksberg, Fyn, Nordjylland, Ribe, Ringkøbing, Roskilde, Sønderjylland, Storstrøm, Vejle, Vestsjælland, Viborg.

CHIEF IMPORTS
Petroleum, machinery, chemicals, textiles, iron, steel, paper.

CHIEF EXPORTS
Food products, fish, general industrial machinery, textiles.

MAJOR RELIGION
Evangelical Lutheran

ROYAL FAMILY
Queen Margrethe II (born April 16, 1940)
Prince Henrik (the prince consort) (born June 11, 1934)
Crown Prince Frederik (born May 26, 1968)
Prince Joachim (born June 7, 1969)

FLAG
White cross on a red background, with the upright of the cross to the left of center.

IMPORTANT ANNIVERSARIES

April 16	Queen's Birthday
May 4	Liberation Eve
June 5	Constitution Day

GLOSSARY

brackish water
A mixture of salt and fresh water, usually close to the coast.

Danelaw
The region in western England colonized by the Vikings.

Fastelvn ("fasta-laon")
The holiday preceding Lent.

fjord
A large inlet from the sea.

folkeskole ("fol-kes-skohla")
A combined elementary and junior high school.

Folketing ("fol-keh-TING")
The Danish parliament.

frikadeller ("FRACK-ah-dil-er")
Meatballs.

hygge ("hoo-ga")
A feeling of warmth and coziness.

Inuit
The native peoples of Greenland.

morgenbrød ("MOHRG-brohd")
Morning bread, one of a variety of breads served for breakfast with cheese or jam.

Nisse ("NISS-ah")
An elf-like person from Danish folklore, now commonly associated with Christmas.

North Atlantic Drift
A warm current from the Gulf of Mexico.

rejsegilde ("RAI-seh-gilder")
A traditional Danish ceremony to celebrate the completion of a new house.

rigsdansk ("rihj-dansk")
Standard spoken Danish, usually spoken by television newscasters.

rolegans ("ROHL-ee-gans")
A word composed of the Danish "rolig" (calm) and the English "hooligans." Applied to Danish soccer fans.

rundstykker ("rond-STOO-kehr")
Crusty rolls.

Scandinavia
The four northern European countries: Denmark, Sweden, Norway, and Finland.

skål ("skohl")
A Danish drinking toast.

smørrebrød ("smehr-brehrth")
An openfaced sandwich.

tak ("tahk")
Thank you, please, excuse me.

wattle and daub
A frame of woven tree branches covered with a paste of straw, mud, and cow dung, used by the Vikings for house walls.

BIBLIOGRAPHY

Best, Beth Wagner. *The Amazing Paper Cuttings of Hans Christian Andersen.* New York: Ticknor and Fields, 1991.

Hintz, Martin. *Denmark.* Chicago: Children's Press, 1994.

Hull, Robert. *Norse Stories.* New York: Thomsen Learning, 1993.

Lerner Publications. *Denmark—In Pictures.* Minneapolis: Lerner Publications, 1991.

Odijk, Pamela. *The Vikings.* Englewood Cliffs, N.J.: Silver Burdett, 1990.

INDEX

INDEX

INDEX

PICTURE CREDITS